# Quick Hits for New Faculty

**DATE DUE**

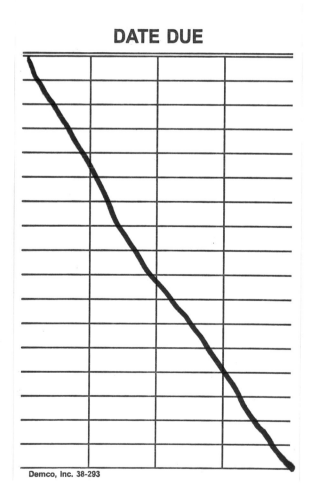

# Quick Hits for New Faculty
## *Successful Strategies by Award-Winning Teachers*

*Editors:*
**Rosanne M. Cordell**
**Betsy Lucal**
**Robin Morgan**

*Advising Editors:*
**Sharon Hamilton**
**Robert H. Orr**

*Illustrations & Layout by:*
*Keith M. Kovach*

This book is a publication of

Indiana University Press
601 North Morton Street
Bloomington, IN 47404-3797 USA

http://iupress.indiana.edu

*Telephone orders*    800-842-6796
*Fax orders*    812-855-7931
*Orders by e-mail*    iuporder@indiana.edu

The paper used in this publication meets the minimum requirements of
American National Standard for Information Sciences—Permanence of
Paper for Printed Library Materials, ANSI Z39.48-1984.

Manufactured in the United States of America

Cataloging information is available from the Library of Congress.

ISBN 0-253-21709-1 (pbk. : alk. paper)

1  2  3  4  5  09  08  07  06  05  04

# Contents

# Introduction

Welcome to *Quick Hits 3*, edited and authored by award-winning faculty, and sponsored by the Indiana University Faculty Colloquium on Excellence in Teaching (FACET). While the first two volumes of *Quick Hits* focused on teaching in general, this volume is aimed primarily at helping new faculty. The articles and strategies range from planning for that first day in the classroom to evaluating student learning to documenting teaching to understanding the politics of teaching and learning in your department and institution.

The title, *Quick Hits*, bears scrutiny. The phrase was coined during the 1991 FACET retreat, when several members of FACET offered some truly engaging but quick strategies for involving students in their learning – a "quick hit" to capture the students' attention. These ideas were gathered together into a volume which captured national attention, and led to the publication of a second volume of "quick hits." While these were successful and useful volumes, we all acknowledge that teaching is much more than a series of "quick hits," and that teaching-learning interactions are ongoing, built on the establishment of credibility and trust, and very much context-dependent. In this third volume, while retaining the notion of engaging students in their learning, we have tried to expand our "quick hits" with additional background information, rationale, and resources. They are, in a sense, not-quite-so-quick hits, but rather ideas that will engage us and our students more deeply.

We have organized this volume in the order that we believe new faculty will need to address teaching and learning issues and decisions. "Chapter 1: Getting Started" discusses the development of a course syllabus, course requirements, and scheduling your own time. "Chapter 2: Grading & Feedback" has ideas on evaluation, assessment, and feedback that are well considered early in your first semester,

preferably as you develop course syllabi and assignments. "Chapter 3: First Day" contains ideas for getting the semester off to a good start. "Chapter 4: Are You Out There?" addresses encouraging and managing student participation. "Chapter 5: Getting Support" offers insight into the many ways in which you can find support for improving teaching and navigating through academia. "Chapter 6: Lessons From the Disciplines" contains teaching tips that, at first glance, seem quite subject-specific, but actually contain ideas that can be adapted to other subject areas. "Chapter 7: Keeping Track" reminds us all that we not only need to do good work, but we also need to document it in ways that will be reflective of the progress and changes we make throughout our careers.

As a new teacher, you may find education to be a daunting task, one that can easily overwhelm. If such is your experience, you are not alone! Teaching is not a simple task and this book is not a "Teaching for Dummies." Quite the contrary, this volume is filled with the wisdom of years of practical experience, experimentation, best practices, research, and so forth. We would hope that you will feel comfortable enough to consider some of these ideas, and we would encourage you to adapt them to your own particular classroom style.

We recognize that not every quick hit will be appropriate for everyone. This is to be expected. Nor is it likely that you will be able to lift a particular technique and apply it successfully without first tailoring it to suit your particular approach to teaching. The important thing is to consider, evaluate, try, and then reflect upon the outcome.

Remember that this volume of *Quick Hits* is but the start of a very important journey for you; a journey that may one day help you to become The Natural as a teacher – the best there ever was, the best there ever will be (with an apology to Bernard Malamud).

# Quick Hits for New Faculty

# Chapter 1:

# Getting Started

*Remember that the reason you teach is because you love it.*
*Your passion for teaching will always come through*
*to your students.*

*Paul Pittman & Doug Barney*

# Truths My Father Told Me

*Catherine Larson*
*Spanish & Portuguese*
*Indiana University Bloomington*

My father retired a few years ago after teaching in the same college for fifty years. Teaching for fifty years is hard to imagine, and it's probably fair to say that during that last year his cognitive skills were not what they once were. Still, I can tell you that he was universally considered the institution's treasure: he was consistently deemed the best instructor on campus and, over the course of half a century, was one of the most active in the areas of research and creative activity. When I first began teaching, he gave me a lot of good advice, and I have tried to build upon his wisdom in the intervening years. What follows is less about what to include in a course syllabus than it is about what he called basic survival lessons. Some are Big Issues and others are small, but individually and collectively, these common-sense ideas can help us get a leg up on how to acclimate to life in academe. Here are some of the basic truths my father told me:

Think often–and reflectively–on the kind of teacher/researcher/colleague you want to be, and consider the myriad ways in which you can achieve those goals. Be prepared to revise your goals and strategies over time.

Watch *assuming* anything. Consult; give things time.

Treat the staff well. They are the ones who make the entire enterprise work well, and they know how to help you. Let them know how appreciated they are.

How do the students in your department address faculty? What messages do forms of address send? Sometimes the little things really do make a difference.

What rhetorical strategies do people use in department and committee meetings? What can you learn from the ways others communicate?

Actively seek mentors and a peer group. You may even want to consider two sets–one from inside your department, and one from outside.

Reflect on the culture of your department and your campus. How do these cultural and political dynamics relate to you and your situation?

Think from time to time about your own professional role models. What decisions were made by the best of the people who influenced you?

Find balance in your life, including balance between your professional and private lives; keep open time to grow intellectually and have a healthy, quality life outside your department.

Within your professional life, make conscious choices about the amounts of time you will be able devote

> **Think often–and reflectively–on the kind of teacher/researcher/colleague you want to be.**

to research/creative activity, teaching, and service. Ask your chair and mentors to recommend reasonable expectations for service, and consider thoughtfully the rewards of service inside and outside the department vs. the consequences of taking on too many obligations. In like manner, think about the ways you can get the most "bang for your buck" in your teaching (and this is intended as a positive statement about teaching)–how can you reflectively and creatively make the time that you devote to your teaching help you achieve your goals and those of your students? In other words, stop occasionally and consider time management issues lest you fall victim to burnout.

Keep the paperwork. Organize files for your annual reports; teaching evaluations; letters attesting to your research, teaching, or service contributions; exemplary teaching projects; etc. It really is true: when it's time to assemble materials for your annual review, tenure or promotion case, or a teaching award nomination, it will be infinitely easier if you know where to find the documentation.

Think about ways to view and talk about our profession in a positive manner. Some academics–we all know the type–have the studied habit of speaking negatively about academe, their students, their colleagues, the administration; the list goes on and on. The ways in which we frame our ideas, handle disagreements, and talk about who we are and what we do say a great deal about us to others, and they surely also affect how we see ourselves.

That's the list, and I know that there's nothing revolutionary in any of it; sometimes we just need to hear it again. I hope it helps. . . .

❀ ❀ ❀

# Getting Started
*Pat Ashton*
*Department of Sociology*
*Indiana University Purdue University Fort Wayne*

**"Covering the Material": Depth vs. Breadth**

How much material should you cover in a given course? The obvious answer is "as much as possible." Given the constraints of time, however, you won't be able to cover everything. Inevitably you will have to compromise as you decide to leave things out. What compromises are appropriate? How much breadth of subject matter should you trade off for going into depth on particular topics? My bias is to err on the side of depth. To speak of "covering all the material" reminds me of painting a wall. Working quickly with a good supply of paint, you can "cover" a lot of wall. But all you have done is to apply a thin layer to the surface of the wall. And although the wall looks really nice immediately after being covered, the paint rather quickly wears off, leaving little trace of either the paint or the painter. An emphasis on "coverage," then, can leave students exposed in the future. But if students become interested and enthused over a relatively smaller number of topics and – more importantly – they learn the methodologies of investigation appropriate to your subject matter, they will always have the motivation and the tools to investigate further. I'm not suggesting that decisions about what to include and what to leave out are not difficult and even painful, but if you design with the end in mind, keeping the focus on what you want students to be able to do with the material, then you will inevitably make good decisions about course organization.

**Some Principles of Good Course Design**

When designing a course – especially when designing one for the first time – it is tempting to begin with concrete features

– e.g., "Let's see….I'll have a midterm and a final exam and maybe a short paper." But this pragmatic approach is short-sighted at the very least, and contrary to the best teaching and learning practices. You should design a course with the end in mind. That is, what do you want students to be able to know and do when they have completed the course? The answer to this question becomes the guiding principle on which all important decisions about the course turn. Below are some questions that will help you identify and stay true to this principle.

**Identify your goal for the course.** How does the course fit into your department, campus, and/or disciplinary curriculum? What are students supposed to get out of taking the course, and what do you expect to get out of teaching the course?

**Develop learning objectives that fit the goal.** The learning objectives should be concrete and stated in clear behavioral terms. This means that each learning objective describes something that students *will be able to do* when they successfully complete the course. Objectives that state "Students will understand…." are not very useful. How will you know that students "understand"? What will students be doing to demonstrate that understanding? The activity of demonstrating understanding – whatever it is – is what goes in the learning objective. Sometimes when you do this you discover that the expectations you have for students are superficial or trivial. This is important feedback; it tells you to throw that material/activity/ objective out or reinterpret your course goal. Instead, some instructors revert to vague learning objectives. But this just means that they are not taking responsibility

for their role in student learning. No wonder students say they are confused about what we're trying to teach them!

**Select assessment tools that fit your learning objectives.** Once you know the behaviors you expect from students, then you can select what activities will best measure those behaviors. And you may find that testing – or at least some kinds of testing – are not appropriate. Or you may find that tests serve an important function in meeting your learning objectives. The important thing is to make sure that everything you ask the students to do is designed to further the course goal.

**Design the course activities to help students accomplish the learning objectives.** Now you have an important measuring stick to make decisions about what goes into a course and what gets thrown out. And you're much more likely to draw students in when you can show them that what they're learning and what they're being asked to do is related to accomplishing course objectives. This is so much more than "teaching to the test" – it's designing teaching and learning with the end in mind!

> **The syllabus for a course represents an implied contract with students.**

## Key Elements of a Course Syllabus

There are, of course, a variety of acceptable styles and approaches to the course syllabus. Some instructors in some courses will keep the goals, objectives, and/or assessments open-ended and subject to collaborative negotiation with students. Others will feel the need to lay out the course in advance. Either way, however, the syllabus for a course represents an implied contract with students. And there are certain things that should be made clear in writing. Here is a checklist:

**Goals and objectives.** Students need to know what the instructor's vision of the course is and what they are going to be expected to learn.

**Assessments.** Students should be given clear guidelines on how they will be evaluated in the course.

**Course Calendar.** Due dates for all assignments should be given. While flexibility is always required, these dates should not be changed lightly.

**Course Policies.** It is important to give students information on rules and regulations that will potentially affect their learning in the course. Possibilities include: attendance policy, including what students should do if they miss a class; classroom decorum, including a statement on civility and respect; definition of plagiarism and how it will be treated; how and where assignments will be turned in and turned back, including policies on late work.

**Student Expectations of the Instructor.** After telling students what you expect of them, it's only fair to let them know what they can expect of you. Possible topics include: enthusiasm, knowledge, availability, organization, major responsibility for the learning environment, extent to which you can/will accommodate disabilities.

**Sources of Help and Support for Students.** This may include tutoring, developmental learning, writing centers, computer consultants. You may want to include room numbers, phone numbers, and websites.

❋ ❋ ❋

# Creating a Syllabus
*Sharon K. Calhoun & Angela H. Becker*
*Psychology*
*Indiana University Kokomo*

The course syllabus is often the first written document you share with your students. Many faculty members view the syllabus as a contract (Altman and Cashin 1992; Smith and Razzouk, 1993), giving information about students' and instructor's responsibilities. Instructors hope that students will use the syllabus (and the instructor's in-class introduction of it) to make an informed decision about whether to take the course and what they must do to be successful in the course. Others (Gunert 1997; Lyons, McIntosh, and Kysilka 2003) advocate for the syllabus as a learner-centered document, whose purpose is to provide information, advice, and tools to help students learn. Their approach is to develop an "extended syllabus," with a table of contents to help direct students to the many pages of information included in the document. The syllabus also serves as a permanent record of the course (Parkes and Harris 2002), and so must contain information to help students, faculty, and administrators make informed decisions about the nature of the course. The dilemma for faculty members is to put enough information in the syllabus to serve all these functions, but not so much that students cannot access the information they need.

Our research (Becker and Calhoon 1999) on students in introductory psychology courses at four Midwestern colleges and universities suggests that students routinely ignore some information included in the syllabus, and that the information they find important varies according to their age (traditional vs. non-traditional) and experience in college (first-semester freshmen vs. continuing students).

Our findings for all students (regardless of age or college experience) were that they viewed the most important items in the syllabus to be those associated with procedures for determining grades: examination/quiz dates, assignment due dates, reading material covered by the exams/quizzes, number and types of exams/quizzes, types of assignments (e.g., readings, presentations, papers), times of required out-of-class events, and class participation requirements. The least important items to these students were title/authors of readings, withdrawal dates, course identifiers (course title and number, etc.) , and the instructor's academic dishonesty policy.

Non-traditional age students, as compared to traditional age students, reported they paid more attention to the kind of assignments a course required and the course objectives, and less attention to policies regarding late assignments and academic dishonesty. First-semester students, as compared to continuing students, paid more attention to the late assignment policy, prerequisite skills and courses, where class materials are located, available support services, and the academic dishonesty policy. Continuing students paid more attention to the types of exams and quizzes and the kinds of assignments that were required by the course.

Given that the syllabus has multiple purposes (contract, learning tool, permanent record), it must contain a fair amount of information. Yet students do not attend well to all of that information. How then can you create a more effective syllabus? We argue that a good syllabus must be student-centered in that it does not overwhelm the student. We believe the syllabus must contain contractual and permanent record information, and that a second document (perhaps a "Student Guide") could contain additional information and learning resources for students.

Therefore, to create your syllabus, we recommend you list all the information you believe students need to make an informed decision about taking your course. Then list information that describes your course to interested third parties (e.g., administrators, review boards, evaluators of transfer students' prior course work). Next, consider what information you believe students need to be successful in your course. Finally, decide which information from these lists would be most useful in the syllabus, and which might be better presented in a Student Guide, course website, or other format.

At a minimum, we recommend the following items be included in your syllabus:

**1. Course identifying information**: List the official course title, number, and section number.

**2. Instructor identifying information**: List your name, position (e.g., Assistant Professor of Biology; Instructor in English), office location, office hours, office telephone number, email address, home phone (if students may contact you at home), and the course website, if there is one.

**3. Required readings**: Although our research suggests students do not attend as much to this item (they probably get this information from sources such as the bookstore's text list), this can be an indication of the scope and depth of the material covered in the course, and therefore is part of the permanent record function of the syllabus.

**4. Course description**: This may be the official course description in the course catalog, but usually is an expanded version of this description. Often this section will include information on prerequisite or co-requisite courses and/or skills. Avoid, as much as possible, using course specific terminology or jargon in this description. It should be understandable to people who are not experts in the field of study covered by the course.

**5. Course goals**: List ways in which your students will be different as a result of having taken your course. Lyons, et al. (2003) recommend one to five broad goals, which may come from any of the three domains of learning: cognitive (changes in thinking), affective (changes in attitudes, ethics and morals, appreciation for beauty or diversity), and/or psychomotor (changes in physical skill). They suggest forming goals by completing this sentence: "As a result of being participating members of my class this semester, students will _____."

Goals are more broadly stated than are objectives. Objectives deal with specific skills and knowledge, and should be measurable. For most courses, you will have several objectives for each unit, which will be tied to your assignments and assessment activities. For instance, you may have an objective for students to be able to describe the processes of classical conditioning and to give an example of how these processes occur in everyday life. To assess whether students have met that objective, you would develop test questions or writing assignments where they would demonstrate their ability to describe and apply the principles. Some authors (e.g., Lyons, et al. 2003) recommend listing your objectives in your syllabus. We believe that listing all the objectives for each unit of the course on the syllabus is counterproductive—we already have problems getting students to attend to some of the important parts of the syllabus, and adding more information would not help.

You may wish to include these objectives as part of the Student Guide, or you may wish to provide them a separate handout or on the course website as each unit is covered.

**6. Course requirements**: This is the section students attend to most. Here you describe examinations, papers, projects, and other activities that students must complete. It is helpful to include how these activities will be graded (e.g., "There will be 3 examinations, each worth 20% of your grade" or "The two research papers are each worth 100 points"). You may wish to include detailed descriptions of each assignment in your syllabus, or you

> **Students viewed the most important items in the syllabus to be those associated with procedures for determining grades.**

may indicate that these descriptions are available in a separate handout, in a Student Guide, or on the course website. To help students find this section quickly, you might include a brief table of assignments that includes assignment title, due date, points/ grade percentage for each assignment.

**7. Grading scale**: If your college or university does not have a standard grade scale, it is likely that different faculty members use different cut-off scores to assign final grades. To avoid misunderstandings (for instance, that grades are arbitrarily assigned), describe how you will calculate final grades. Include how much each assignment is worth (either points or percentage of final grade), and what the cut-off scores are for each letter grade.

**8. Course schedule**: Create an organized , easy-to-consult list with date, topics, and assignments for each class period. If your course is organized around a textbook, list the chapter titles as well as chapter numbers. This will be useful in cases where students need to demonstrate course equivalence, for instance, if they transfer to another college or university. This is also helpful if you teach a course that is a prerequisite for another course on campus; you can share your syllabus with the instructor(s) of that course to ensure that your students are gaining the knowledge and skills needed in the more advanced course. Also, list the dates of scheduled breaks and holidays, as well as withdrawal dates, to assist students in planning their semester.

Once you have developed your syllabus, how can you help students attend to it? We recommend that when you first present the syllabus to your students, give them time to find the information they deem the most important (likely all the information pertaining to how they will be graded). Be willing to clear up any questions or concerns about those things first. Then the students will be ready to listen to you when you talk about the information you believe is most important for their learning. Raymark and Connor-Greene (2002) recommend quizzing students over the syllabus, to help them attend to the information contained in it.

In our research, we found that students tend to pay less attention to many items on the syllabus as the semester proceeds. For example, in comparing students' end-of-semester reports and beginning of- semester reports, we found that students paid less attention to makeup and late assignment policies, as well as academic dishonesty policies, near the end of the semester. This is when students have assignments due in several of their classes, and they may be tempted to skip a quiz or turn in a late (or "borrowed") assignment in your class. We recommend you remind students of your policies for late assignments and make-up work, as well as penalties for academic dishonesty, a few weeks before the end of the semester. In addition, our students paid less attention to the goals and objectives of the course at the end of the semester. If you have scheduled a comprehensive project or examination, remind your students of the goals you listed in the syllabus a few weeks before that assignment is due, and describe how these goals relate to the final project or exam.

Finally, be aware that students are often overwhelmed during the first week of classes. As a new faculty member you might be able to relate to this. One of us conducts the new faculty orientation sessions on our campus. I was approached by a new colleague at mid-semester, who was frustrated that she was getting phone messages from students who had missed class. They wanted to know how to get their assignments to her. "It's in my syllabus! They shouldn't be calling!" The faculty member then asked how to make long distance phone calls. This just happened to have been discussed in the new faculty orientation session at the beginning of the year. I pulled out a handout from the orientation packet and went over it with her. She said she had forgotten that this was covered in orientation, thanked me, and left. About an hour later, she returned, saying, "I just want you to know that I got the irony of that!" As you build your syllabus, consider that students will not remember everything you put in it, and will be grateful for gentle reminders to review the information throughout the semester.

**References:**
Altman, Howard B. and William E. Cashin.
1992. Writing a syllabus. *Idea Paper*
27. Manhattan: Kansas State
University, Division of Continuing
Education, Center for Faculty
Evaluation and Development.

Becker, Angela H. and Sharon K. Calhoon.
1999. What introductory students
attend to on a course syllabus.
*Teaching of Psychology* 26: 6-11.

Grunert, Judith. 1997. *The course syllabus:
A learning-centered approach.*

Bolton, MA: Anker Publishing. Lyons,
Richard E., Meggin McIntosh
and Marcella L. Kysilka..
2003. *Teaching college in an
age of accountability.* Boston:
Allyn and Bacon.

Parkes, Jay and Mary B. Harris. 2002. The
purpose of a syllabus. *College
Teaching* 50: 55-61.

Raymark, Patrick H. and Patricia A. Connor-
Green. 2002. The syllabus quiz.
*Teaching of Psychology* 29: 286-288.

Smith, Mary F. and Nabil Y.Razzouk. 1993.
Improving classroom communication: the
case of the course syllabus. *Journal of
Education for Business* 68: 215-221.

❋ ❋ ❋

# Top 10 Practices that Lead to Student Success
*Paul Pittman & Doug Barney*
*Business & Economics*
*Indiana University Southeast*

Do you feel your students do not have a common understanding of what it takes to succeed in college classes (and in life)? Have you ever had students come to you only after earning a poor grade on an exam or assignment, wanting suggestions on what they can do to improve their performance? Having been a successful student yourself, there is little doubt you have ideas about what students should do to be successful, yet you may never have put these ideas into concrete statements. We have developed a list below that you can share with your students at the start of the semester. The authors suggest that sharing this "Top Ten" list with students at the beginning of the semester will benefit students by constructively challenging their understanding of what they can do to improve their learning and success. The ten items listed here are not all-inclusive and your list may vary from this one. The list below is a combination of ideas that we share with our students at the beginning of each semester to create a common understanding of how they can be successful. These ideas can be shared with students in a variety of different ways, including PowerPoint, overheads, or on the syllabus. Both professors emphasize the importance of these concepts on the first day of class and devote sufficient time for this discussion.

**Here is the top ten list we share with our students (in bold), including a brief explanation of each item:**

**#10 – How we use our time shows what we value.** If you feel rushed, it's because you likely are. Today's environment, with its many distractions, including cell phones, internet connections, and anticipation of instantaneous feedback, can impel us to expect to get more done in less time. We increasingly feel the pressure to be available 24/7. Prioritize your time appropriately. If you wish to do well in your academic pursuits, plan to work at it and conscientiously allot time consistent with those pursuits.

**#9 – It's not easy, but you can be successful if you choose.** The choice is yours. Make the most of it. If you want to excel, or even just pass, you must put "time on task." This means specifically schedule time each week for your academic pursuits. Time estimates vary, but expect to work on material about 2 to 4 hours outside class for every hour in class. Aim higher than the mark you want to hit. If your goal is to "just pass" the course, that will be the *highest* level of performance you can achieve and it is likely you will end up not passing. Learning is maximization rather than minimization. Because life is full of uncertainties, it is better that we aim high and fall short rather than aim low and fall short. For example, if you had to be at an important meeting at 10 am tomorrow and this meeting was at an office located two hours away, almost everyone would suggest leaving more than two hours in advance to assure they arrive on time. The more important it is that you arrive on time and/or the more uncertainty you have in getting there on time, the earlier in advance you would leave. This same logic works for learning.

**#8 – If you get behind, you will likely never catch up.** Why? We are too busy! Furthermore, material covered in most courses is cumulative, resulting in less understanding of the new material covered.

This can become a vicious cycle. Get the jump on your courses early and keep up. Prepare by studying (not just reading) the material before every class.

**#7 – If you are repeating the course and do the same things you did before, do not be surprised if you have the same results.** What is even worse is the false assumption that you know the material when you see it again. Familiarity is different from learning and understanding. 'Nough said.

**#6 – Study the material thoroughly before every class.** If you don't study the material before class, you will only truly get about 50% of what the class covers, but you will think you got 100%. This is especially true for good teachers who can explain material well. Studying the material includes reading the material, reflecting, and exploring the material further when you do not thoroughly understand it. If the class requires or suggests homework, attempt it (without looking at the answers until after you thoroughly finish your attempt) before class. Remember, we learn most from our mistakes, which is precisely what homework is for. Do not assume that you can simply watch the professor do something in class and then be able to do something similar on an exam without attempting it yourself first. For example, I watched Tiger Woods in several tournaments last year and read several golf publications. How hard could this be? I thought. So I decided to become a professional golfer. After about two holes I discovered that I was not a professional golfer. Why? Two reasons. I had not practiced for years like Tiger Woods and, perhaps, I do not have the natural ability for the sport. The same is true of academic pursuits. You must study hard to do well, and if the discipline in question is not one

**Teaching/learning is a process.**

11

in which you excel, you will need to study even harder than the average student just to do as well as the average student. Frequently, students who earn the highest grades are NOT the brightest; rather, they are choosing to be and are committed to being successful.

**#5 – You must study all the assigned material.** The class will not cover all the material on which you will be tested nor will the class go over all the homework. Your allotment of enough time outside class is essential to course performance.

**#4 – Teamwork happens** in the workplace, too. In fact, teamwork is a growing phenomenon in all successful organizations because we can learn both collectively and from each other. Take advantage of your peers as a resource. Form study groups and work together. Not only will you find new friends who are committed to the same objectives, you end up with partners that can help to motivate you when you are discouraged. Learning occurs as a result of exercising your brain, similar to fitness occurring as a result of exercising your body. Consider your peers as exercise partners for both your mind and body.

**#3 – Open your mind to new ideas.** Openness is a prerequisite to inquiry and learning. This is especially difficult when you feel that you don't agree with the ideas expressed. Learning does not require agreement with others. Respect and professionalism is a basic characteristic employers expect in college graduates. Likewise, it should also be practiced in the college classroom. Professionalism includes recognizing and acknowledging the contributions of others (i.e., not plagiarizing) and respecting their views. It also includes observing the Golden Rule –"Treat Others as You Would Have Them Treat You."

**#2 – Class attendance does not guarantee academic success**; but it is a minimal requirement for academic success. Similarly, just because you go to work every day does not mean you will be successful on the job. You must also practice the guidelines discussed above to provide further assurance of academic success.

**#1** – Drum roll please... **"I can't learn you the material."** Learning is a deeply personal process that happens within an individual because they choose for it to happen. In other words, learning is not a passive process for the learner. While I (the teacher) may do the best possible job of creating an interest while presenting material (e.g. lecture, teamwork, role-playing, etc.), it is the responsibility of the students to learn the material. Success is your (the student's) responsibility. [Note to faculty: As a teacher, be willing to accept that you will not get through to all the students. If you attempt to reach every student, you are unlikely to provide the best educational experience to other students. We all have a limited amount of time.]

Teaching/learning is a process. In this process, there are strengths and weaknesses. Even if we as teachers were able to overcome all of our weaknesses, there are still going to be limitations in facilities, students' innate abilities, and student's desires to learn. We must accept this inevitability and do our best. Remember that the reason you teach is because you love it. Your passion for teaching will always come through to your students.

If you want to learn more about motivating your students and using motivational tools and setting goals in class, check out *Punished by Rewards*, by Alfie Kohn. We also recommend *Schools that Learn*, by Peter Senge, which re-examines our current educational systems and how they influence learning. Specifically, Senge discusses how learning can be improved through enhancing intrinsic (e.g., individual desire) rather than extrinsic (e.g., grades) motivators. According to Senge, extrinsic motivators alone will not suffice. He argues all people are born with an innate desire to learn. Schools currently focus too heavily on providing extrinsic motivators, mainly rewarding and punishing via grades.

**References:**

Kohn, Alfie. 1993. Punished by rewards: *The trouble with gold stars, incentive plans, A's, praise, and other bribes.* New York: Houghton Mifflin.

Senge, Peter M.. 2000. *Schools that learn: A fifth discipline fieldbook for educators, parents, and everyone who cares about education.* New York: Doubleday Press.

❋ ❋ ❋

# Engaging Students in the Development of the Syllabus

*Valerie N. Chang*
*Social Work*
*Indiana University Purdue University Indianapolis*

Many authors recommend developing a classroom atmosphere characterized by respect, mutuality, collaboration, and open dialogue (Knowles 1980; Nagda et al. 1999; Rudd and Coming 1994) so that students will be comfortable being active participants in their learning (Cramer 1995; Freire 1970, 1974, 1985; Haynes and Beard 1998). The classroom climate should invite collegiality and be perceived as safe and supportive. The classroom atmosphere must be grounded in equitable relationships rather than imposition, intimidation, or privilege (Goodrich 1991). Creating such an atmosphere can be a challenge, particularly when many students have learned to be passive and receptive rather than active and involved. The process of using students' ideas to redesign the syllabus or course plan is an excellent way to begin inviting active collaboration in the learning process.

If you believe that instructors and students are both actively involved in the teaching learning process, then contributions from students are important in determining course structure and design, assignments, and grading methods (Graham 1997). Before each semester I write a syllabus that lists course objectives, explains course assignments, outlines class topics and assignments, includes a list of relevant references, discusses grading and evaluation, and gives important details such as course policies. By necessity this course plan is developed before I meet the students and hear about their learning needs. After going over the syllabus, I invite students to think about previous learning experiences and identify several themes related to their learning. First, I ask them to think about how they learn. Do they learn best by reading, by listening, by doing something, by talking? Then I ask them to identify what kinds of assignments have been the best learning

> **Using students' ideas to redesign the syllabus is an excellent way to invite active collaboration in the learning process.**

experiences. Finally I ask students to review in their minds ways they have been evaluated and to identify those ways that have promoted the most learning. Was it weekly quizzes, final exams, papers, presentations, group projects, etc.? Having completed this personal review, I ask students to form small groups and share with each other how they learn and what kinds of assignments and evaluation systems have promoted the most learning. A recorder in each group summarizes their discussion to share with the class when we come back together.

In their small groups, I also ask them to review the course objectives and pick the three or four objectives that are most important to them as a group. Each group reviews the assignments and can make recommendations about alternative assignments that might better meet their needs. The group reviews the points given to each assignment and when the assignment is due. They can recommend changes in any of these aspects of the syllabus. If there are particular aspects of the syllabus or assignments that I am not willing to change, I explain why those aspects or assignments cannot be changed.

When the groups complete their deliberations, each group summarizes their discussion on the board, lists the most important objectives, and writes any recommendations for changes in the syllabus. After each group has reported to the whole class, we discuss what teaching methods they find most effective, identify the objectives identified as most important, talk about assignments that will lead to achievement of these objectives, and consider what portion of their grade each assignment or project
should be worth. The class works together to develop agreement on any changes in assignments or evaluation plans. Sometimes, however, I allow students to select among various assignments that all have the same point value.

When groups recommend giving assignments different point values, the whole class has to work out some acceptable plan that has the agreement of at least the majority of the students. When considering evaluation procedures, they generally compromise on some broad variety of methods such as oral presentations, papers, take-home exams, and in-class exams. If necessary, I make adjustments to improve the learning atmosphere.

This process gives each student a voice in making decisions about the class and communicates that I believe they can make valuable contributions to the course. This practice conveys my respect for students' opinions and knowledge, my willingness to work cooperatively with them, and my expectation that they will work together . Doing this process on the first day of class helps to establish a climate of flexibility, openness, and collaboration and increases students' sense of ownership and involvement in their learning.

**References:**

Cramer, E. P. 1995. Feminist pedagogy and teaching social work practice with groups: A case study. *Journal of Teaching in Social Work* 11 no.1/2: 193-215.

Freire, Paulo. 1970. *Pedagogy of the oppressed.* New York: Seabury.

Freire, Paulo. 1973. *Education for critical consciousness.* New York: Seabury.

Freire, Paulo. 1985. *The politics of education.* New York: Continuum Press.

Graham, M. A. 1997. Empowering social work faculty: Alternative paradigms for teaching and learning. *Journal of Teaching in Social Work* 15 no.1/2: 33-49.

Haynes, D. T. and N. C. Bard. 1998. A collaborative teaching model to build competence. *Journal of Teaching in Social Work* 16 no.1/2: 35-55.

Knowles, Malcolm Shepherd. 1980. *The modern practice of adult education from pedagogy to andragogy.* New York: Cambridge.

Nagda, Biren A., Margaret L. Spearmon, Lynn C. Holley, Scott Harding, Mary Lou Balassone, Dominique Moise-Swanson and Stan de Mello. 1999. Intergroup dialogues: An innovative approach to teaching about diversity and justice in social work programs. *Journal of Social Work Education* 35 no. 3: 433-449.

Rudd, Rima E. and John P. Comings. 1994. Learner developed materials: an empowering product. *Health Education Quarterly* 21 no.3: 313-327.

❊ ❊ ❊

## Reflect, Refine, and Refresh

*Lori Montalbano-Phelps*
*Communication*
*Indiana University Northwest*

Teaching is both rewarding and challenging. A collaborative method of teaching and learning requires that there is reciprocal relationships of trust and respect for the teacher and students. As I develop courses, I find it very helpful to allow for flexibility in the syllabus, so that the course can evolve and adapt to the particular personality of the class. I have found, from many years of teaching multiple sections of the same course, that each class unfolds differently. Some classes involve students who are engaged by the discussion and experiential style of learning. They prefer a "hands-on" approach to learning. Other classes seem to require more guided approaches to teaching, including lecture, or more application exercises, and so forth. Because of the differing needs and interests of the specific group of students that constitute a class, the syllabus has to offer options to the instructor so that adaptions can occur. We all remember the instructor who rigidly stuck to the syllabus and, whether we had time or understood the material, we marched forward. This rigidity often leaves students behind, students who could benefit from a more relaxed approach. Ultimately, flexibility allows for greater growth and understanding. While learning a great scope of material is good, if it is learned and forgotten after the exam, it loses its value.

To remain flexible, I will put in two or three "catch-up days" in the syllabus, so that if students need extra time with the material, we can work it in. These days aren't necessarily identified as catchup days in the syllabus itself, but are often centered on classroom activities that are expendable if necessary. For example, I might write in the syllabus "video presentation and analysis" for a given class meeting. Time allowing, I'll show the video. If we need to cover past material, that would probably become the priority for that day instead. Also, there is nothing wrong with revising a course somewhat while you are in the semester. Minor changes, which reflect the needs of the class, are often considered more helpful than problematic. At the end of each syllabus, I provide a disclaimer, which states, "any of

> **The syllabus has to offer options to the instructor so that adaptions can occur.**

this syllabus subject to change."

I do not recommend changing course requirements significantly. After all, the syllabus is like a contract between you and your students. During the first few days of class, they learn what your expectations are, and measure whether they are willing or able to make the commitment. Significant changes in requirements, particularly adding major requirements can be unsettling, and students may react negatively.

Finally, self-reflection is a must. Teaching often requires adapting to changing student populations, a changing world, and changing viewpoints by a specific group of students. It requires that courses evolve from semester to semester for applicability and significance for the students. After the end of a semester, when I begin to re-think a course or prepare for an upcoming semester, I will ask myself, did we meet the objectives that are contained in the course description and/or syllabus? Why or why not? Were the students actively involved in the course development? What material needs to be added, what material has become less important? How effective was I at teaching this topic? How can I improve? What worked well in the course? And so on. This type of reflection is not only helpful but also necessary to continually meet students' needs. Reflection doesn't have to mean chastising yourself. If there was a problem, deal with it: reflect on what can be done to avoid the problem the next time. Build on past success. Refine yourself and the course.

**References:**
Austin, Ann E. and Roger G. Baldwin. 1991. *Faculty collaboration: Enhancing the quality of scholarship and teaching*. Washington D.C.: George Washington University Press.

Braskamp, Larry A. and John C. Ory. 1994. *Assessing faculty work: Enhancing individual and institutional performance*. San Francisco, CA: Jossey-Bass.

Grasha, Anthony F. 1996. *Teaching with style: A practical guide to enhancing learning by understanding, teaching and learning styles*. Pittsburgh: Alliance Publishers.

Halpern, Diane F. 1994. *Changing college classrooms: New teaching and learning strategies for an increasingly complex world*. San Francisco, CA: Jossey-Bass.

Light, Greg and Roy Cox. 2001. *Learning and teaching in higher education: The reflective professional*. Thousand Oaks, CA: Sage.

McKeachie, Wilbert J. 1994. *Teaching tips: Strategies, research, and theory for college and university teachers*. 9th ed. Lexington, MA: D.C. Heath.

Weimer, Maryellen and Rose Ann Neff, eds. 1990. *Teaching college: Collected readings for the new instructor*. Madison, Wisconsin: Magna Publications.

❋ ❋ ❋

# Staying Sane in Academia

*Robin Morgan*
*Psychology*
*Indiana University Southeast*

For the first several years that I taught, I found myself inundated with massive numbers of tests and papers to grade at both midterm and during the final two weeks of the semester. Like most of my colleagues, I teach three courses per semester with 30 to 45 students in each class. As a result, I would spend hours trying to read each paper thoroughly and calculate grades before the registrar's deadline. The notion of getting these tests and papers returned to the students in a timely manner as advocated by the literature on teaching (see, for example, Chickering & Gamson, 1991) seemed ludicrous.

Finally, a light dawned. As I reviewed my previous semesters' syllabi in preparation for creating new syllabi, I discovered what should have been obvious. In each class I taught, the due dates for papers were within the same week. Likewise, exams were scheduled during the same five to seven day period. I was the one creating the mess for myself!

How to fix this problem? First, rather than giving exams and a final paper in each course I teach, I look for assessment activities that fit my course objectives and allow for a more staggered approach to grading (see, for example, Walvoord, Bardes, and Denton 1998). This resulted in two changes:

1. More frequent grading of smaller assignments. For example, in my introductory course I might assign four out-of-class essays that are due throughout the semester. None might be due in the final week of the course.

2. Assignments tailored to course objectives rather than always relying on exams and term papers. For example, in one of my advanced courses students must present diagnostic criteria of various disorders. These presentations occur throughout the semester with only one or two students making a 3-5 minute presentation each class day.

Second, at the beginning of each semester I coordinate due dates across my courses so that assignments are due at different times. By simply aligning the due dates and exam dates of the courses as I create the syllabi, I have eliminated the midterm and end-of-the-semester craziness. Now, I am able to provide students more immediate feedback on their assignments as I am only trying to grade the assignment from one course at a time. In addition, my students, my colleagues and my family have a more sane and relaxed individual with whom to interact!

**References:**
Chickering, Arthur W. and Zelda F. Gamson, eds. 1991. *Applying the seven principles for good practice in undergraduate education.* San Francisco: Jossey-Bass.

Walvoord, B.E., B. Bardes and J. Denton. 1998. Closing the feedback loop in classroom-based assessment. *Assessment Update* 10 no.5: 1-4.

❋ ❋ ❋

## Scheduling Special Events

*Rosanne M. Cordell*
*Franklin D. Schurz Library*
*Indiana University South Bend*

While you are putting together the syllabi for the courses you will be teaching, give some thought to the types of special events you want to include in each course–guest speakers, library instruction sessions, field experiences, etc.–and schedule with the appropriate people BEFORE you finalize your syllabi. You are more likely to get the dates that work best for you if you schedule well in advance, and you can more easily fit into your class schedule the types of activities that make these special events most useful to your students, such as assigning readings before a guest speaker, or discussing research assignments and approving topics before a library instruction session. For field experiences, you may also need time to arrange transportation or get paperwork submitted. Most people are more than willing to help you bring special events and resources to your students and appreciate your giving them enough notice to prepare adequately.

❋ ❋ ❋

# Chapter 2:

# Grading & Feedback

*"Knowing what you know and don't know focuses learning."*
*Chickering and Gamson (1991)*

## Course Participation and Self-Grading

*Betsy Lucal*
*Sociology*
*Indiana University South Bend*

In my upper-division courses, I include attendance and participation as a portion of the students' final grades. Because of the difficulty of keeping track of students' attendance and contributions to course discussions, and as a way of taking student personality and other factors into account, I ask students to fill out a form that I then use to assign this grade. The form asks them to estimate how many classes they missed over the course of the semester, how many of those absences they think should be excused and why. I then ask them to rate their participation in the class on a scale of one to ten and, again, to explain why. Finally, I ask them to assign themselves an overall grade for attendance and participation (one to ten scale) and to explain why. This form serves several goals. It gives students a chance to provide input on the grade they think they deserve; and it offers them the opportunity to reflect on their performance on this aspect of the course. It reminds me of, and alerts me to, good and bad reasons for students' missing my class. It lets them tell me if they are generally shy or otherwise reluctant to speak up in class. I tell students that people who attend class every day but never talk will not get an A for attendance and participation, nor will they get an F. I've found that students generally do a good job of rating their performance; students are prone to give themselves a lower grade than I would, rather than to overestimate their grade (though that does happen).

✳ ✳ ✳

## Measuring and Assessing Class Participation

*Paul Pittman and Doug Barney*
*Business & Economics*
*Indiana University Southeast*

Many faculty encourage and formally reward class participation due to the understood value that class participation has in the learning process. There are, however, two primary factors that faculty struggle with in awarding credit for class participation. These two problems areas are developing formal criteria for assessing individual participation and sharing these criteria with students. This Quick Hit is an attempt to help faculty address these two problems.

The following includes a syllabus excerpt and discussion that provide a foundation for class participation. We recommend a discussion of class participation at the beginning of the semester and we revisit the importance of participation as needed throughout the semester. The last part of this teaching tip provides an instrument for assessment of participation.

**Pedagogical Technique and Class Participation:**

    Class attendance and participation are extremely important to the understanding of course material and to generate meaningful dialogue from which we all can learn. Therefore, students are expected to attend class on a regular basis AND class participation will account for 15% of the total grade earned in the course.

    Class participation is an essential part of this course and, therefore, valued and rewarded. Unfortunately, grading class participation is necessarily subjective. The key criterion for evaluating effective class participation for this course include:

    1. Does the participant attend class regularly? Is the participant prepared? Do comments show evidence of analysis of the material? Do comments add to our understanding of the situation? Does the participant go beyond simple repetition of the facts? Do comments show an understanding of the theories and concepts?

    2. Is the participant a good listener? Are the points made relevant to the discussion? Are they linked to the comments of others? Is the participant willing to interact with other class members?

    3. Is the participant willing to test new ideas or are all comments "safe?" Is the participant an effective communicator? Are the concepts presented in a concise and convincing fashion?

    Class participation involves articulating clearly your position and supporting it, and also the willingness to seek alternative perspectives. Participation enables you to learn from your colleagues and to help them learn from you. Good class participation is not simply repeating the facts, monopolizing class time, second guessing the instructor, or ignoring the contributions of fellow participants. Simply talking for the sake of being heard is not valued and the class is expected to help with people who seem to be insensitive to the learning process.

**Implementing this Technique:**

To assist in the evaluation of class participation, students use the last 10 minutes of class time each week to provide comments regarding the strengths and opportunities for improvement for the class and time for self-assessment. (See the assessment instrument below.) Class feedback is used to make real-time changes throughout the semester to improve the class, rather than being solely reliant on end-of-the-semester student-evaluation feedback. A short summary of student comments can be shared with the class each week along with a discussion of how concerns will be addressed. Second, students rate their own class participation as good, average, or poor while supporting their self evaluations with illustrations of how they contributed to that night's class meeting (e.g., constructive contributions to discussions such as comments, outside materials, etc.). This self-assessment is their evaluation on a 0/1 scale of 13 participation items and should include a reflective discussion of how they can improve their participation.

To convert these self-assessments into course points, two aspects are considered – the actual quality of a student's participation and whether the students' self-assessment includes constructive reflections on how they plan to improve their participation. Part of this assessment also includes follow-up on whether the student actually does improve their participation, based on their self-assessment. It is important to remember that the objectives are to have active class participation, honest self-assessments, and continuous improvement. All three of these components are necessary to have constructive class participation.

A total of 3 participation points are available for students to earn each week, which are ranked on a simple scale of zero for no attendance, 1 for poor participation, 2 for average participation, and 3 for good participation. The percent of total participation points that the student receives during the semester out of the total participation points available is then converted to the course points allotted for participation. For example, if 50 course points are allotted to participation and the student received 26 of the 36 participation points available, then the student receives 72% of 50 for course participation points.

To learn more about the value of participation, readers might refer to *Educators*

*as Learners: Creating a Professional Learning Community in Your School*, by Wald and Castleberry (2000). In this work, the authors outline tools and techniques for creating a learning community. We also recommend Bonwell and Eison's (1991) work for its guidance on how to elicit involvement by students in discussion and keep them interested, even when the subject matter of a course is generally uninteresting. Our discussion of participation is also consistent with Conlan's (1998) techniques for structuring and providing guidelines for student behavior in the classroom.

**Class feedback is used to make real-time changes throughout the semester to improve the class.**

**References:**
Bonwell, Charles and James Eison. 1991. *Active Learning: Creating Excitement in the Classroom*, New York: Wiley Publishing.

Conlan, Vanessa. 1998. Managing with Class: Effective Classroom Techniques. *The Teaching Professor* 12, no.10.

Wald, Penelope and Michael Castleberry. 2000. *Educators as Learners: Creating a Professional Learning Community in Your School*. Association for Supervision and Curriculum Development, Alexandria, Virginia.

Name _____                    Date _____

**Class meeting:**

Strengths:

Opportunities for improvement:

My participation:
1 for YES, 0 for NO:            0 to 4 is POOR
                5 to 9 is AVERAGE
                10 to 13 is GOOD

                                                    Did I attend? _____
                                                    Was I prepared? _____
                Did my comments show evidence of analysis of the material? _____
                Did my comment add to our understanding of the situation? _____
                                Did I do more than just repeat the facts? _____
        Did my comments demonstrate understanding of the theories and concepts? _____
                                            Was I a good listener? _____
                        Were the points I made relevant to the discussion? _____
                        Were my comments linked to the comments of others? _____
            Did I demonstrate my willingness to interact with other class members? _____
                        Did I demonstrate my willingness to test new ideas? _____
                                        Did I communicate effectively? _____
                        Did I communicate in a concise and convincing fashion? _____
                                            TOTAL SCORE FOR TODAY _____
                                            RESULT: _____

**Personal Reflections** :

❈ ❈ ❈

# Learning by Teaching

*Leah Savion*
*Philosophy*
*Indiana University Bloomington*

The culture of disconnection that undermines teaching and learning, says Parker Palmer (1998) in the famous book *The Courage to Teach* is driven in part by our Western commitment to think in polarities. The distinction between the teacher (the sage on stage with all the answers) and the student (the obedient recipient of knowledge) may be beneficial in some domains, such as driving and open-heart surgery, but it fails to be effective in academic settings, where the goal is to turn students into thinkers and not merely containers of information.

Effective learning, not being a spectators' sport, calls for active participation of the learner in the process. Perhaps the ultimate in active learning required for real learning takes place when the student plays (temporarily) the role of a teacher. The benefits of incorporating appropriate teaching techniques that render your student into a (temporary) teacher include:

**Reduction of well embedded misconceptions** that normally inhibit the acquisition of the academically sanctioned theories and explanations.

**Familiarity with one's own learning styles**, and possibly the development of cognitive flexibility, such as moving from the serialistic style to the holistic style when coping with new material.

**Development of metacognitive skills**: awareness of one's approach to problem solving, monitoring of the process, and revising unsuccessful methods when necessary.

**Critical awareness of diverse (even wrong) approaches**, which enriches one's understanding of complex material, and helps prevent future mistakes.

**Understanding of different levels of understanding**, e.g., as demarcated by the abilities to summarize, criticize, analyze, synthesis etc.

**An appreciation of the distinction between knowing and being able to teach properly**, and of the role of the instructor as facilitator of comprehension via active learning.

The following suggests four distinct techniques or settings of enhancing learning through "learning by teaching":

| TEACHER | STUDENT | METHOD |
|---|---|---|
| 1. Student | Peer | In-class study groups |
| 2. Expert | Novice | Out-of-class tutoring |
| 3. Insider | Outsider | Teach the lay-person |
| 4. Student | Teacher | Enlighten the Teacher |

**STUDENT** groups are best formed by the students without the instructor's intervention, with the single restraint of being able to meet outside of class at least twice a week. To cement the existence of these groups as learning units outside of class, some group assignments can be incorporated into the final grade. Group mates are responsible for each other's understanding, they are expected to help each other to cover lost material and to prepare for tests, and are encouraged to rotate the role of the "writer" and the "teacher" among them.

**OUT-OF-CLASS TUTORING** is a remarkably successful device, in which everyone wins. Lower class (e.g., introductory class in your field) students can ask for a free tutor by handing the teacher a note with their e-mail address; the notes are then distributed among the upper-class volunteer students, who provide three tutoring units (60-90 minutes each) for some extra-credit points.

**TEACH THE LAY PERSON** takes place when a difficult concept or distinction is conveyed in class, or when an explanation for a theory or a phenomenon tends to contradict "common wisdom", creating a contrast with commonly held naïve misconceptions. The students submit a detailed report about their teaching assignment: who was the student, how did they detect his confusion about the topic at hand, what methods did they use for explaining the difficult point, and how they tested their student for comprehension. Of all methods for reducing the effect of prior false beliefs and of incorrect approaches on learning, "teach the lay person" seems most effective.

**TELL ME SOMETHING NEW** is a requirement the instructor can make concerning the mid-term or the final paper. The tables are turned when the teacher asks the students to teach her something she does not know or hasn't thought about. Students tend to get very excited when given such an opportunity. They engage in long conversations with the instructor, attempting to find out what areas in their studies (within or outside the field) they can branch into for their term paper, and make connections with material covered in class in innovative ways that will impress and enlighten the teacher.

Turn your students into momentary teachers, sit back in your chair, and watch them in action. The least of all possible impacts of any of these strategies is an unmistakable wave of admiration for the

difficulties you encounter and overcome everyday in your profession.

**References:**
Palmer, Parker. 1998. *The courage to teach: Exploring the inner landscape of a teacher's life.* San Francisco, California: Jossey-Bass.

❊ ❊ ❊

## Using Students to Provide Prompt Feedback
*Jamie Kauffman*
*Speech Communication*
*Indiana University Southeast*

When teaching students how to evaluate sources of information in public speaking, I have students practice in class by evaluating hypothetical sources of information. Students must receive prompt feedback on their in-class practice efforts in order to learn this critical thinking skill. They need to know what they're doing correctly and what they still have yet to master. I've found that I can use fellow students to provide feedback within the same class period. Here's how I use formative peer assessment.

I give students a hypothetical source of information and ask them to evaluate it using criteria we have discussed in previous classes. The criteria:
1. Accuracy: is the information redundant, verifiable, and recent?
2. Relevance: does the information come from an expert in the area, a person, group, or organization in a position to know?
3. Objectivity: is the source of the information non interested--not in a position to benefit from making claims?
4. Sufficiency: is the information complete?

26

I ask the students to place their names on the top of their papers. I collect the student answers and then redistribute them to another class member. Next, I ask students to evaluate the paper they have received in an effort to help a fellow student find out what that student does and does not know before the student will be graded on this skill. I use an overhead with the "correct" answer to explain, criterion by criterion, the four criteria for evaluating sources of information, explaining how students should have applied each criterion to the source of information in determining its worthiness. As I explain, students assess the paper before them, providing feedback as to which answers are incorrect and why. As I review each criterion, I ask the student evaluators to hold up a hand if the paper they are evaluating has a correct response for that criterion. In so doing, I enable students to see how the class faired on applying each specific criterion.

Once I've explained each criterion and the students have provided feedback, I ask the "evaluator" to place his or her name at the bottom of the paper. I then collect papers and return them to the authors. I ask the students to read the feedback they received and to note what they did correctly and what they did incorrectly. I encourage students to review outside of class the criteria they didn't understand and/or did not apply correctly. Finally, I collect the papers. Before the next class period, I review the papers and the feedback to ensure that student assessors provided correct feedback. If I find that the original response and/or the feedback are incorrect, I make certain that I point this out to the author and/or evaluator. In my experience, students haven't been reluctant to provide such formative evaluation since they want to help their fellow students perform well on tests,

and they know that the feedback they are providing is not part of a grade.

As Chickering and Gamson (1991, 66) state, "knowing what you know and don't know focuses learning. Students need appropriate feedback on performance to benefit from courses." The authors add that "no feedback can occur without assessment. But assessment without timely feedback contributes little to learning." Pedagogically, using formative peer assessment to provide prompt feedback has at least two benefits. First, it enables students to get feedback on their work within the same class period. As Benson, Mattson, and Adler propose (1995, 58), "prompt feedback is generally better than postponed feedback." I would never be able to provide such feedback during the same class period to a large number of students. Second, formative peer assessment reinforces the correct answer by requiring students to review answers and to assess another student's effort. "By having students provide feedback on each other's work, students sharpen their own critical thinking skills, as well as their ability to articulate feedback in an appropriate manner," write Benson, Mattson, and Adler (1995, 58). "Providing feedback to others allows students a chance to reevaluate their own work after having experienced the work of others." The authors add that it is essential that instructors explain the criteria and expectations to the class *before* the students attempt to assess the efforts of their classmates.

Prompt feedback is essential to learning. Yet, providing such feedback can take a great deal of time and energy. Using peer evaluation of in-class work not only allows for a quicker response than I can provide, but it also reinforces student learning of a skill or the course material.

**References:**

Angelo, Thomas A., and , K. Patricia Cross. 1993. *Classroom assessment techniques: A handbook for college teachers,* 2d ed. San Francisco: Jossey-Bass.

Benson, D, Lu Mattson, and Les Adler. 1995. Prompt Feedback. In *The seven principles in action: Improving undergraduate education,* ed. Susan Rickey Hatfield. Bolton, Massachusetts: Anker.

Chickering, Arthur W., and Zelda F. Gamson eds. 1991. *Applying the seven principles for good practice in undergraduate education.* San Francisco: Jossey-Bass.

LeClercq, Terri. 1999. Seven Principles for Good Practice in Legal Education: Principle 4: Good Practice Gives Prompt Feedback. *Journal of Legal Education* 49, no.3: 418-29.

✳ ✳ ✳

## So What's Your Grading Philosophy?
*Robert H. Orr*
*Computer Technology*
*Indiana University-Purdue University Indianapolis*

### To Grade or not to Grade

We live in a society that is obsessed with tests and competition – all as part of an effort to be considered "fair." We test children early and often and sustain that practice into their adult years, be it in college or in industry. The results of the testing and subsequent grading influence future performance in what is often referred to as the Pygmalion Effect (Latzko and Saunders 1995). The effect is a kind of self-fulfilling wish or prophecy. Good students tend to continue to do well; poor students continue to struggle, as in, "I can't do math," or "I hate writing – I'm just no good at it." So, the next time you grade a student's work, consider the impact that grade will have on the student's subsequent performance.

Interestingly, an impromptu survey of several outstanding teachers suggests most would refrain from grading students in more advanced courses. This same group suggested that grading was necessary to motivate younger students to attend and actively participate in class.

But what is a grade really? Some will suggest it is the teacher's way of assessing student performance, but that belief presupposes a close tie-in between what the student is expected to learn (teaching objectives) and what the student is asked to demonstrate (testing activities). Grades can also be used to measure progress – plotting a path of continual improvement, monitor declines in overall performance, identify areas of concern, and so forth.

Each of us must develop our own grading philosophy. Not only must we decide numeric cutoff scores if we use quantitative assessment measures, but we must establish meanings for each type of grade possible, decide what to grade and what not to grade, develop assessment instruments, publish grading standards, avoid trivializing the process, be sensitive to grade creep or grade inflation, decide whether to grade on a curve...the list seems never ending; yet each of these issues impacts on a grading philosophy that will become uniquely yours, a philosophy that will evolve out of these and related issues as you learn to grapple with them.

### Grade Inflation/Grade Creep

Although related, these two terms are

not identical. *Grade creep* is a statistically measurable phenomenon that suggests a slow, but generally steady increase in grade point averages for an aggregate of students representing some academic unit. For instance, if the mean Grade Point Average (GPA) of all sophomores in a particular school ten years ago was a 2.60 and today, a similar measure from the same school yielded a mean GPA of 2.65, we would conclude that the mean GPA had *crept* upwards by 0.05 points. This is not necessarily a bad thing. The increase might well be the result of improved teaching methods or better admission practices.

*Grade inflation* on the other hand, suggests a cheapening in the meaning or value of an assigned grade (see the discussion on the meaning of grades below). Suppose that ten years ago, twenty percent of all algebra students received an A for their efforts and today at the same institution, sixty percent of all algebra students received an A. Although one might make the same "improved teaching" argument as with grade creep, the magnitude of the increase is so dramatic that we are more likely to conclude that the letter grade 'A' no longer means the same thing today as it did ten years ago. The grade has somehow been cheapened.

Grade inflation and grade creep exist. They should both be monitored and faculty should be encouraged to discuss possible explanations openly. Getting a better understanding of each phenomenon is the first step in being able to exert some degree of control over them. Should safeguards be imposed to prevent their occurrence? I would be reluctant to endorse them.
Suppose for example, we limit the number of A's and B's to a combined forty percent of the total number of grades assigned per course. Such a tactic would likely keep both

grade inflation and grade creep in check, but at what cost? How can we keep students motivated to do their best if the majority are going to receive grades of C+ or less? Quota systems are aggravating to both students and teachers, so why have them?

**Assignment of Grades**

Since the ultimate goal of assignment grading is to produce an assessment record that can be applied relatively easily to calculate a final course grade, we will now examine what actually can be involved in assigning grades for individual assignments.

First of all, we will address the *reward* vs. *punishment* aspect. Receiving a good grade can be perceived by both students and faculty as a reward for an assignment well done. Indeed, assigning a good grade can be the teacher's way of expressing an appreciation for the hard work demonstrated by the student. Likewise, a bad grade can often be perceived as a punishment for a poorly executed assignment. There is nothing wrong with either perception, but there are dangers that lurk. As teachers, we must ensure not only that each grade is earned, but also that the grade is not influenced by our personal feelings or biases toward the student. It is easy for us to say that "each student got what he or she deserved," but can we always be sure that we are being totally objective?

One professor acquaintance insisted that his students place their name in the upper right corner on the reverse side of the last page of an examination. In this way, he never knew the identity of the student whose work he graded until after all questions had been scored. Certainly this action underscored a belief that the assignment of grades could raise ethical issues. Dare we grade good students more gently and poor students more harshly? It is a difficult task to always grade fairly and impartially. Yet that is precisely what we must do if we are to retain our credibility with students and colleagues alike.

**Grade Rubrics**

These can be either quantitative or qualitative depending mainly on the teacher's preference. True, certain types of assessment instruments lend themselves readily to either one method or the other, but this is not an absolute. For example, in a mathematics course, it might seem that evaluations would be based primarily on examination performance in which the

examination consists of a set of problems, the computed answers to which are either correct or incorrect. Such a test would lend itself readily to a quantitative scoring rubric (90 – 100% = A and so forth). Likewise, a test consisting of all multiple choice questions is designed for easy quantitative scoring. However, a mathematics teacher could be quite creative in posing questions

that require explanations of methods rather than computations, which would give greater flexibility in determining a grade. The questions can now be graded more subjectively. For example, Laker and Farnum (2001), in their development of a grading rubric for an electrical engineering design course taught at the University of Pennsylvania, proposed the following:

## EE-441 GRADING CONSIDERATIONS

| ITEM | A | B | C | D / F |
|---|---|---|---|---|
| Theoretical Design | Mostly Complete | Partial | Vague | Little |
| Calculations | Significant | Some | Negligible | None |
| Artwork | More than Required | Required Amount | Some | Insignificant |
| Preliminary Results | Yes | Yes | No | No |
| Understanding of Remaining Tasks | Clear | Partial | Vague | Little |
| Schedule | On Track or Slightly Behind | Needs Minor Revision | Needs Major Revision | Completion Questionable |

Note how the grading is based on a series of items for each assignment, and that the letter grade definition has become far more subjective. These qualitative rubrics require much thought and grading is more difficult. For example, at what point does *partial* understanding become *clear* understanding? Still, subjective scales tend to allow students greater freedom in presenting their mastery of concepts.

Ultimately, we must evaluate the effectiveness of the rubric. Does it work or is there some deficiency that needs to be corrected? The assessment of the rubric is closely related to the assessment of grade standards that appears below. Anticipate that shortcomings will exist, and even when the rubrics prove successful, they may still fail in the future simply because no two groups of students behave identically.

**So What Do Those Grades Really Mean?**

As a continuation of the discussion on rubrics, we next address the issue concerning the meaning of the letter grades given at the completion of the course. If we settle into the more "traditional" interpretation of letter grades (A is excellent or outstanding, B is above average, C is average, D is below average and F is unsatisfactory), we create an interesting dilemma for ourselves. If a grade of C is to be considered *average*, then statistically, we should expect more of this type grade than any other – regardless of the collective abilities of our students. If you were to survey grades from an academic unit or institution, you might not find such a trend. What may have once been true is no longer the case.

In court cases, students have asserted that since they were paying for the course, they should not have their employment

prospects jeopardized by non-competitive grades. Indeed, at one time, such prestigious universities as Harvard, MIT and Stanford permitted students to retake a course as many times as they wished until they attained a grade with which they were happy (Orr et al. 1995). At IUPUI, a survey of all undergraduate student grades for an entire semester revealed that the mean GPA for sophomores was 2.7; for juniors, 3.0; and for seniors, the mean GPA was 3.3 (Orr 1995). Intuitively, we recognize that the relative frequency of C grades could not have been dominant. Our earlier supposition of *average* may have been too simplistic and also obsolete.

Hogue (2003) defined a C grade as follows: "Student has met most teacher/course expectations. Progress has been slow, but adequate. The student needs to re-evaluate his/her goals and devise a strategy to engage in higher expectations." Hogue further suggested that the B grade reflected students as having met all teacher expectations. Clearly, the C grade carries a derogatory stigma whereas the B grade does not.

The Environmental Studies faculty at the University of Waterloo defined the (C, C+, C-) grade as: "The student has demonstrated some understanding of subject matter, can assimilate and communicate basic aspects of the subject matter. The work is of satisfactory or adequate quality according to evaluation criteria," (Undergraduate Studies Committee 1984). Again, there seems to be a derogatory stigma attached. Their definition of the B series of grades is quite detailed: "The student has shown good comprehension of subject matter, evidence of critical and creative thought, familiarity with literature and previous work in subject area, competence in communication and presentation skills, but none of the above to the degree found in [the] A category. The work is of very good quality according to evaluation criteria," (Undergraduate Studies Committee 1984).

The accompanying sidebar demonstrates a well-thought-out definition of the letter grades (Schramm 1999). Regardless of whether your department, school, campus, or university sets an interpretive standard for letter grades – or whether you must compose one yourself, the other side of the equation relates to the performance standards you establish. If your standards are set too low (that is, they are easily attainable), then too many students will receive A and B grades. Conversely, if your standards are set too high, they are unattainable, and the result will be a proliferation of Cs and Ds. Thus, the standards and the interpretive meanings must work in harmony, and this is not easy to do.

# The Meaning of Grades*

### A: Excellent/Mastery
Excellent work demonstrating thorough preparation, genuine comprehension and synthesis, insight, and even originality. It is remarkably well-written and presented. The grade signifies not simply very good work but exceptionally fine work.

### B: Good/Competent
Very good, thorough work. The work demonstrates *thorough* preparation, a grasp of the subject matter, and a *thorough* command of the materials of the course. It may not show any special insight or originality, but it demonstrates clear understanding of the material with comprehensive answers presented in a clear and logically correct style.

### C: Acceptable/Satisfactory
The work is acceptable for degree credit. It does not mean "poor" work because we should not award degrees for poor work. The work demonstrates an adequate, though not comprehensive, grasp of the subject matter. For example, significant information might be overlooked; the work may not display a full appreciation of the meaning or implication of a question; answers might be too brief to allow sufficient development; an essay might read as a list of facts rather than a well-developed argument; it might appear to be derived wholly from lecture material, ignoring relevant readings or references to the readings. Though imperfect, the work is, on the whole, of a quality that is acceptable in the sense that the award of the degree for this level of work is warranted.

### D: Poor but passing
Work that only barely qualifies for academic credit. The student has clearly learned something from the course, but the work is shoddy and shows poor or inconsistent preparation. The general impression is of an examination or essay that is inadequately prepared or understood and poorly presented. A student who performs consistently at this level should not expect to be awarded a college degree.

### F: Unacceptable
Work that shows little or no preparation or comprehension. For example, many facts or references are missing or are misunderstood; there is little or no analysis, and the style is poor, confused or incomprehensible. A student can attend classes (or at least some or most of them), do the reading (perhaps inconsistently), and hand in the required work and yet not produce a product that reflects a command of the materials of the course.

*Derived from Professor Peter W. Schramm, Ashland University

## The Consequences of Grading

In our opening paragraph we suggested that grades have consequences. Whether grades have significant consequences might be a matter of conjecture and might well be dependent upon the individual psyche. Still, Deming labeled grades as one of his Forces of Destruction of individual performance. As early as kindergarten, a child might receive a gold star for an "excellent" finger painting. But what of those children who fail to receive the gold star? Are they already branded as "no good in art" (Latzko and Saunders 1995, 28)? Deming thought so and certainly my own experience would provide anecdotal reinforcement of that notion. Parents can exacerbate the grading situation by criticizing the failure to earn a gold star (later on this becomes, "why did you only get a C in English? Are you dumb or just lazy?"). By the time the student comes to college, the grade force of destruction has had nearly a lifetime to take hold. Perhaps the best we can do with any performance that fails to meet our expectation is to find some good to build on and help the student to improve and fulfill his or her potential. Encouraging feedback can work to begin to change the student's outlook and self-perception.

Good grades have consequences as well. They, likewise, can be reinforcing of "good behavior" in that the student receives confirmation of continued excellence. However, we cannot conclude that students who have met or exceeded our expectations have thus fulfilled their potential. Nor can we conclude that we have nothing further to teach them. Although we spend much time commenting on the work of those who fail to meet our expectations, we have an equally important opportunity to comment on the work of good students. In addition to verbal kudos, we can proffer questions that will extend their responses into areas of inquiry not yet explored. In other words, for every correct answer, there is always another question. Challenge the good students never to rest on their laurels but to continue to study. This is potentially our greatest legacy as teachers.

It is especially important that good grades be truly reflective of a student's work. Our credibility and the credibility of our institution are at stake here. If a student receives an A in an advanced writing course, and then proceeds to demonstrate to an employer an utter inability to write a cohesive paragraph, the employer begins to form a low opinion of the school from which the

> **Challenge good students never to rest on their laurels but to continue to study.**

student graduated. Bear in mind that a final assessment of our abilities as teachers as well as the effectiveness of our university may not occur until some years after our students graduate. Daunting prospect, that!

## Grade Standards

Whatever we decide on the meaning of grades, we must publish our rules for computing final course grades. Students expect this and certainly have a right to know how they will be graded. Of perhaps equal importance, do not change these standards during the course. To do so is to violate a covenant you have made with your students. There will be times when you will be unhappy with the distribution of grades your standard produced. Accept that and wait until you next teach the course to revise your standard. If you must, you can reserve the right to *lower* your standard if it appears to be too difficult

33

– students won't object to that – but *never* raise that standard for a course, even if you realize the standard was too easy to achieve. You have a teaching lifetime ahead of you to "get it right."

I strongly discourage the use of targets or quotas being appended to your grade standards (not more than 20% of the students can receive an A, and so on). Such a practice creates an internal competition in which students vie with each other for top honors. While I have nothing against competition, in the case of the target method students generally do not know where they stand until the course is completed. Likewise, grading on a curve can be considered a mathematically clever yet devious way of establishing targets.

Students presume that to grade on a curve means that standards may be lowered if the class as a whole does poorly on the assignment. There are professors who use *standard normal* or *z-scores* as the basis for computing letter grades. Student who are two standard deviations above the class mean will receive an A. The problem with this technique is that we return to the old notion of average – recognize statistically that half your students will be below average regardless of how well or how poorly everyone is doing. We still have students competing with each other, and more importantly, as a teacher, you have failed to really define in practical and meaningful terms what your letter grades mean.

There are some who will debate this last point about grading on a curve by suggesting that they consider all students to whom they ever taught this course to as their population base. Although this would allow for a particular class to be collectively above average, population norms can vary because you, as a teacher, have changed and your student preparedness for your course has changed over time. There are too many biases to suggest a stable population.

My advice therefore is to create subjective levels of achievement as your standards. By far this is the more difficult approach, but you will become a better teacher and your students will have a more realistic understanding of what you expect from them.

**Conclusion**

Just as your teaching philosophy will evolve over time, so will your grading philosophy evolve. But overall, your grading philosophy will be based on everything that we have discussed thus far. Add to this mix, the notions of what is ethical or morally right to you, what is fair to the students, and finally, what feels right. Developing a grading philosophy takes time and careful consideration. Feel free to discuss this matter with your colleagues and by all means, share your philosophy with your students.

**References:**

Hogue, Dawn. *CyberEnglish9 Policies*. 2003. Sheboygan Falls, Wisconsin: School District of Sheboygan Falls; available from http://www.sheboyganfalls.k12.wi.us/cyberenglish9/Business/grade%20philosophy.htm. Accessed 15 August 2003.

Laker, Ken and Philip D. Farnum. 2001. *EE441 and EE442: EE Senior Design, 2000-2001*. Philadelphia: University of Pennsylvania; available from http://www.seas.upenn.edu/ese/ee442/presentations/vgexample/VGexample.pdf. Accessed 15 August

Latzko, William J. and David M. Saunders. 1995. *Four Days with Dr. Deming: A strategy for modern methods of management.*. Reading, MA: Addison-Wesley.

Orr, Robert H., Margaret Applegate, Mark Grove, Sandy Hellyer, Norman Douglas Lees and Kimberly Quaid. 1995. Report on Grade Inflation at IUPUI. Indianapolis: Indiana University Purdue University Indianapolis.

Schramm, Peter W. 1999. *The Meaning of Grades.* Ashland, Ohio: Ashland University; available from http://www.ashland.edu/colleges/arts_sci/polysci/syllabi/1999fall/ 101_schramm.html. Accessed 15 August 2003.

Undergraduate Studies Committee, Faculty of Environmental Studies. 1984. *Guidelines to the Meaning of Grades.* Waterloo, Ontario Canada: University of Waterloo; available from http://www.ahs.uwaterloo.ca/~jthomson/grade.html. Accessed 15 August, 2003.

❋ ❋ ❋

# Testing: If You're Going to Do It, Do It Right

*Pat Ashton*
*Department of Sociology*
*Indiana University-Purdue University Fort Wayne*

Testing is without a doubt the most frequently used method of assessment in education. I think that this is more because it is the most familiar method, not because it is the best. Often, I think, other methods of assessment – papers, projects, presentations, etc. – make more sense as a way for students to demonstrate mastery of the course objectives. Tests have their place, but if you're going to use them, do it right. Here are some principles for the appropriate design and use of tests.

**Tests should cover important, nontrivial material.** Objective tests, in particular, have earned a reputation among students as "mickey mouse, multiple guess" phenomena. This is largely due to the fact, I believe, that many of these tests include questions that exist simply because it was easy to put some course-related information in that format, not because this was the most important information for students to master. Beware of selecting questions from computerized test banks without carefully reviewing each one. I have found many questions to be invalid measures of learning. Many others remain at the level of recognition, instead of requiring students to engage in higher-level learning skills like analysis, application, synthesis, or evaluation. Essay questions, too, can be trivial or stated in terms so vague and general that they are extremely difficult for students to answer successfully. Ultimately, tests should allow students to demonstrate mastery of important concepts.

**We should prepare students to be successful on tests.** As instructors, we are responsible for ensuring that students have the resources to perform well on tests. Why should tests be occasions for students to have to play "Guess what the instructor is thinking"? We need to clearly identify in advance what material students need to know for the test. And we need to cover that material in the course as well as give students practice in demonstrating mastery in the same way they will be required to do on the exam. There is no angrier confrontation between student and instructor than the one with the student who feels that they were tricked, deceived, or set up for failure. Too often, they are right, although the instructor might not have intentionally done so. We can avoid this problem by connecting the learning to the class pedagogy and both of these to the exam.

**Tests should be learning experiences, too.** Tests should be more than just a way to give students a grade. When test questions are designed around higher level learning skills like analysis, application, synthesis, and evaluation, they do just this. Also, test questions can and should be inclusive. That is, the situations and characters that appear in the questions should reflect the diversity of American society. Not every question should be about "John and Mary." Students should always have a way of getting feedback on the test and have an opportunity to find out why their answers were determined to be correct or incorrect. Without this crucial step, the test becomes mere hoop-jumping to get a grade.

❋ ❋ ❋

# Chapter 3:

# The First Day

*Instructors who create a comfortable atmosphere that stresses active learning are likely to succeed in involving a greater number of students in discussion.*

*Jay Howard*

# The First Class: Making an Impression

*Pat Ashton*
*Department of Sociology*
*Indiana University-Purdue University Fort Wayne*

Right or wrong, first impressions are lasting impressions – and, they are generally accurate. So why wouldn't we want students to have the impression of our course as an interesting exploration of important subject matter taught by a knowledgeable, enthusiastic, and student-friendly instructor? Yet many instructors defeat this purpose by simply handing out the syllabus and letting the students out early. While most students seem to respond positively to being let out of any class early, on a deeper level, they are bound to be a little disappointed. Is the instructor excited about teaching this course, or are they just going through the motions? Don't miss this opportunity to make a positive impression of you, your course, and your subject matter. While the actual content of what you do will vary by subject matter and your teaching style and personality, I would suggest that, at the very least, you demonstrate your enthusiasm for this course and its subject matter. Share with the students why you are teaching this course, and why you are interested in this subject matter. Enthusiasm (and the lack of it) is contagious. If students see that you are looking forward to teaching this course, then they are likely to look forward to taking the course. If your course design includes demonstrations, small group discussions, collaborative learning, other media, etc., consider including some of them on the first day. This not only gives students an accurate taste of what the rest of the course will be like, but it allows students who prefer to learn in other ways a chance to make other scheduling choices.

> **Right or wrong, first impressions are lasting impressions.**

## The First Class: Sharing Expectations and Concerns

In my upper-level courses especially, I pass out 4"x 6" index cards to the students during the first class period. I use them differently depending on the course. In some courses, I ask the students to write down their expectations by completing the following phrases: From this course I expect...; From the instructor I expect...; From my fellow students I expect...; From myself I expect...Students then volunteer their answers and I write them under the matching response category on the board. We then discuss which expectations can realistically be met within the framework of the course, and who is primarily responsible for meeting them. This not only allows specific connections among students and between students and the instructor, but it also propels me to make modifications to the course to meet student expectations where possible. Further, I sometimes incorporate these cards into a final course assessment. At the end of the course, students must go back and reread the card they filled out at the beginning and discuss whether they met their expectations and how they did so. It is a valuable kind of self-reflection that I encourage students to do in all of their courses.

In courses where students come in with some sort of dread (in sociology, usually the theory and methods courses), I have students write on the cards (anonymously) what they want to get out of the course and what their biggest concern is. I then collect and shuffle the cards and pass them out again. The students read the card they were given and pass it to their left. They go on reading and passing until each student has read every card. Then I elicit common themes and put them up on the board. I find that this technique goes a long way toward allaying the students' concern that "I'm the only one who feels this way." This technique also allows every student's "voice" to be heard. If I simply had a discussion in which I asked for volunteers to share their concerns, not everyone would speak up. But by sharing every card, everyone's response is heard. This technique can be used as well in other situations in which it is important to hear from everyone – e.g., in a discussion of certain controversial issues or incidents.

❀ ❀ ❀

## Classroom Discussion Norms

*Jay Howard*
*Sociology*
*Indiana University-Purdue University Columbus*

Sociologists have long been interested in social norms. Norms are simply rules, be they formal or informal, for behavior in particular situations. Often norms are taken for granted to such an extent that we only notice them when they are violated. For example, whenever we board an elevator, we turn and face the doors. It is a habit so ingrained that we don't even think about it. But imagine if you were riding on an elevator and someone else boarded and then stood facing the rear of the elevator. You'd probably be getting off at the next floor!

The college classroom is rife with norms that guide students' and instructors' behavior. Most often we take these norms for granted. We all recognize that students tend to sit in the same seats class period after class

period even when there are no assigned seats. We also expect that students will enter the classroom and take a seat facing the front of the room. We don't expect to have to wrestle the podium away from students!

There are also some very ingrained norms regarding participation in discussion in the college classroom. For example, Karp and Yoels (1976) suggested that one norm in the college classroom is that students are expected to pay "civil attention." Paying "civil attention" differs from "paying attention" in that civil attention involves creating an appearance of paying attention rather than actually paying attention. How do students create this appearance of paying attention? They do so by nodding their heads, making occasional eye contact (but not for too long – which risks the instructor calling on them!), jotting something down on paper, chuckling at our attempts to be humorous, and so on. They may well be daydreaming, writing a shopping list, or wondering what to have for lunch, but they have fulfilled their classroom obligation by creating an appearance of paying attention.

How do students get away with paying civil attention in the college classroom? They do so because there is another college classroom norm that says the instructor will not call on any student who does not wish to be called on. We have an unspoken agreement with our students. We don't call on and risk embarrassing them and they won't challenge us too directly or too vociferously. Of course, there are some exceptions to this norm. Frequently in math and foreign language classes, students are called upon to solve problems or answer questions. But most of the time, a college student can avoid participating in class discussion without fear of being embarrassed. This, of course, also provides students with a license to skip homework and reading assignments.

Karp and Yoels, borrowing from Goffman (1963), point out that students tend to see the college classroom as an unfocused interaction instead of a focused interaction. In a focused gathering, participants are required to interact. In an unfocused interaction, participation is optional. The result of students' definition of the college classroom as an unfocused interaction is the "consolidation of responsibility." In their research on student participation in classroom discussion, Karp and Yoels discovered that, regardless of class size, a handful of students (5 to 8) account for the vast majority of student contributions to classroom discussions. My own research conducted at Indiana University-Purdue University Columbus shows that the consolidation of responsibility is alive and well (see Howard, Short and Clark 1996; Howard and Henney 1998; Howard and Baird 2000; Howard, James, and Taylor 2002).

Sometimes, as faculty members, we think we have done a sparkling job of facilitating discussion in class. But with careful reflection, we may discover that only a few students participated in the discussion to any significant extent. What really happened was a dialogue between the instructor and the five to eight students accepting the consolidation of responsibility with the rest of the class primarily playing the role of spectator.

Why should instructors care if only a small number of students are participating in discussion? College students are adults, after all. Should we be forcing them to participate if they are uncomfortable doing so? One could argue that we make students "uncomfortable" in lost of ways: giving exams and quizzes, assigning difficult or challenging reading, requiring writing and rewriting, etc. Why should requiring discussion be any different? However, there are better reasons for involving students in classroom discussion. Research on student learning suggests that students who actively participate in discussion learn more than students who remain passive in the classroom (see for example, Astin 1985; Johnson and Johnson 1991; Kember and Gow 1994; McKeachie 1990; Meyers and Jones 1993). Participation in discussion also helps develop students' critical thinking skills (Garside 1996; Smith 1977). Instructors can also use classroom discussion to lead students through different levels of learning (Bloom 1956; Brookfield 1995; Steen, Bader and Kubrin 1999).

In addition to being aware of the tendency for only a small number of students to participate, we also need to be aware that not all types of students participate equally. Older students are much more apt to assume the role of "talker" in class, while younger students remain passive "nontalkers" (see research by Howard). The evidence on student gender is mixed at best. Some early studies suggested that female students were somewhat less likely than males to participate (for example, Brooks 1982). Other more recent studies, particularly in classrooms with a wide range of student ages, have failed to find such an effect (see for example, Constantinople, Cornelius and Gray 1988, Howard, Short and Clark 1996). Instructors who create a comfortable atmosphere that stresses active learning are likely to succeed in involving a greater number of students in discussion (see for example, Nunn 1996). Juniors and seniors are more likely to report being "talkers" than are freshmen and sophomores and students who sit in the front third of the room are more likely to be talkers than students in the back two-thirds of the room (Howard, James and Taylor 2002). We know that only a small number of students will chose to be talkers and we have an idea of which students will assume this role. However, we are left with the question, why do some students become talkers, but not others? How do talkers and non-talkers perceive the classroom differently?

When Howard, James and Taylor (2002) asked students about what they perceived to be their responsibilities, talkers and non-talkers agreed that they should attend class, complete assignments, pay attention, learn the material, study, and ask for help when needed. The one responsibility they disagreed on was participation in class discussions. Talkers were significantly more likely than nontalkers to agree that speaking up in class was a student responsibility. As Karp and Yoels noted, nontalkers tended to see the classroom as an unfocused interaction wherein participation was purely voluntary. Howard and Baird (2000) found that students invoked the "student as customer" analogy to justify their lack of participation. Students stated that they were paying to hear the professor talk, not to hear themselves or their classmates talk. Clearly, we have some work to do in convincing students that they can contribute to their classmates' learning and vice versa.

In examining students' reasons for their lack of participation, non-talkers are more likely than talkers to say "I don't know enough about the subject matter," "my ideas are not well formulated," "I am shy," "someone else will do it," "the class is too large," and "the course is not interesting to me" (Howard, James and Taylor 2002). These reasons point to a need for faculty who want to encourage greater participation in discussion to give non-talkers an opportunity to reflect prior to speaking up. Such classroom assessment techniques as the

two minute paper and think-pair-share (see Angelo and Cross 1993 for these and other ideas) allow quieter students an opportunity to reflect and gather their thoughts which can make them feel more comfortable participating in discussion. If instructors don't allow for such reflection, the talkers will continue to assume responsibility for discussion in the college classroom and the non-talkers will gladly let them. Instructors may need to intentionally and directly seek to "slow down" the participation of the talkers. For example, instructors can create an opportunity to involve more students by saying, "let's hear from someone who hasn't spoken up yet," or "someone from the back of the room." Instructors can also put students into smaller groups to encourage their participation. Then students can be asked to report back from their group, making participation a bit safer for students who may lack confidence in their own responses.

In sum, consolidation of responsibility will very likely be the norm in your classroom unless you actively seek to redefine your classroom in such a way that it is apparent that this norm does not apply in your class. The first day of class is very important for establishing classroom norms, so instructors need to start at the very beginning of the class to establish a norm of participation for all students (see for example, Haas 1994). We need to become scholarly teachers who systematically seek to take advantage of the research literature on teaching and learning to facilitate our students' learning. One starting point is to consider what scholarship tells us about the domain wherein we most frequently interact with students – our classrooms.

> **Encourage greater participation in discussion to give non-talkers an opportunity to reflect prior to speaking up.**

**References:**

Angelo, Thomas A. and K. Patricia Cross. 1993. *Classroom assessment techniques : A handbook for college teachers*. 2d ed. San Francisco: Jossey-Bass.

Astin, Alexander W. 1985. *Achieving educational excellence*. San Francisco: Jossey-Bass.

Bloom, Benjamin Samuel, ed. 1956. *Taxonomy of educational objectives; Cognitive domain*. New York: Longmans, Green.

Brookfield, Stephen D. 1995. *Becoming a critically reflective teacher*. San Francisco: Jossey-Bass.

Brooks, Virginia R. 1982. Sex differences in student dominance behavior in female and male professors' classrooms. *Sex Roles* 8: 683-90.

Constantinople, Ann, Randolph Cornelius and Janet M. Gray. 1988. The chilly climate: fact or artifact? *The Journal of Higher Education* 59: 527-50.

Garside, Colleen. 1996. Look who's talking: A comparison of lecture and group discussion teaching strategies in developing critical thinking skills. *Communication Education* 45: 212-27.

Goffman, Erving. 1963. *Behavior in public places*. New York: Free Press.

Haas, Linda. 1994. Generating discussion from the first day. In *Quick hits: Successful strategies by award winning teachers*, ed. Eileen Bender, Millard Dunn, Bonnie Kendall, Catherine Larson and Peggy

Wilkes,12. Bloomington, Indiana: Indiana University Press.

Howard, Jay R., George James and David R. Taylor. 2002. The consolidation of responsibility in the mixed-age college classroom. *Teaching Sociology* 30, no. 2: 214-234.

Howard, Jay R. and Roberta Baird. 2000. The consolidation of responsibility and students' definitions of the college classroom. *The Journal of Higher Education* 71: 700-721.

Howard, Jay R. and Amanda L. Henney. 1998. Student participation and instructor gender in the mixed age college classroom. *The Journal of Higher Education* 69: 384-405.

Howard, Jay R., Lillard B. Short and Susan M. Clark. 1996. Student participation in the mixed-age college classroom. *Teaching Sociology* 24: 8-24.

Johnson, David W., Roger T. Johnson and Karl A. Smith. 1991. Cooperative learning: increasing college faculty instructional productivity. *ASHE_ERIC Higher Education Report No. 4*. Washington, D.C.: George Washington University.

Karp, David A. and William C. Yoels. 1976. The college classroom: Some observation on the meaning of student participation. *Sociology and Social Research* 60: 421-39.

Kember, David and Lyn Gow. 1994. Orientations to teaching and their effect on the quality of student learning. *Journal of Higher Education* 65: 58-74.

McKeachie, Wilbert J. 1990. Research on college teaching: The historical background. *Journal of Educational Psychology* 82: 189-200.

Meyers, Chet and Thomas B. Jones. 1993. *Promoting active learning: Strategies for the college classroom.* San Francisco: Jossey-Bass.

Nunn, Claudia E. 1996. Discussion in the college classroom: Triangulating observational and survey results. *The Journal of Higher Education* 67: 243-66.

Smith, Daryl G. 1977. College classroom interactions and critical thinking. *Journal of Educational Psychology* 69: 180-90.

Steen, Sarah, Chris Bader and Charis Kubrin. 1999. Rethinking the graduate seminar. *Teaching Sociology* 27: 167-173.

✳ ✳ ✳

## The First Day of Class – Don't Waste a Minute

*Teesue Fields*
*Education*
*Indiana University Southeast*

I once overheard two students talking in the cafeteria prior to the start of classes. One was lamenting the need to miss the first day in one of his classes because he had to cover a shift at his job due to an ill coworker. His companion said, "Oh, don't worry. Nothing ever happens in the first class. It will probably only meet for a few minutes. You won't miss anything."

This sentiment is echoed by a number of students and since these students were speaking from experience, it is clearly also a belief of many college professors. But the literature on teaching indicates that the first day of class may be the most important day of class because it sets the tone for the rest of the semester (Felder 1995; McKeachie 1994).

There are a number of important things that can be accomplished in the first session. In fact there are so many, that there is probably not enough time to do everything. The teacher will need to decide what the priorities are for this particular class.

### Right Time, Right Place: Logistics

Before the first day of class I go by the room I am teaching in and check it for equipment and room arrangement. Many of my classes are in the same building and I am familiar with them, but even in these rooms the chairs or tables are often rearranged in a way that does not fit my teaching. Usually that means I will need to get to class early on the first day and arrange the seats, set up my audio visual equipment and generally get things ready for class. This makes me look organized and prepared and creates the favorable first impression I stress to my students! I always make a list of things I want to be sure to take to class on the first day (such as note cards for the students to fill out), to minimize the chance I will forget something.

### Do as I Do: Modeling Positive Behavior

Although parking problems and finding rooms can cause students problems in the first days of class, I always start class on time. I want to model the behavior I will use during the entire semester and communicate that if students are late they will miss something. Because I get to class early, I have an opportunity to talk with students as they come in and sort out if they are in the

44

right location. Usually I have a power point slide on the screen saying, "Welcome to Education G500," so students can just glance in the door to check on the class name.

After I give a few words of welcome, I talk about rules for the class. Since I am in the School of Education, one thing we always stress to K-12 teachers is that classroom rules need to be explicit or there will be more anxiety for the students. As well as modeling the behavior, I also want students to be sure of the rules. So I talk about absences, food and drink in class, talking in class, raising a hand to answer, turning cell phones off, etc. And I let them know we will start class on time and will usually meet for the entire period.

### Yes, You Have To: Setting Expectations

We know that students come into many classes with a great deal of anxiety (Perlman & McCann, 1999). This may be based on reputation (they've heard it's the hardest class in the department) or just their own personal anxieties ("I never do well in discussion type classes"). One thing the teacher can do is to discuss openly what the class is and what it isn't. When I am teaching a required class, I try to explain why this class is important and how it is going to fit in with their major and benefit the students' understanding of the subject. If it is an elective course, I try to be very explicit about what the class is designed to cover (and what it won't cover), so that students can change classes if the disconnect is too great. I find that clearly discussing the expectations saves a lot of griping on the end of the semester reviews concerning why the class did or didn't meet the student's needs.

I also try to explain why they have to do certain assignments in the course and how these fit the course goals. Often I will relate student testimonials from previous classes, indicating that yes, the assignment was difficult, but it was also very rewarding. If the class has a reputation of being difficult, I try to explain why this is necessary and the amount of help I will offer to anyone having trouble (for instance private help sessions or chances to redo certain projects). Students seem to really appreciate knowing that they will have multiple opportunities for help.

Finally, I explain why I have chosen to teach the course. I try to convey my enthusiasm for this particular course and why I enjoy teaching it. (The first day is definitely not the time to share negative opinions about course assignments by the dean!). I convey a sense of hope and tell them how much I look forward to working with them and getting to know them.

### What am I Doing Here: Sharing Personal Information

Students like to know personal information about their instructor. I give them some of my academic background and experience in education and counseling (graduate students in education always want to know whether or not you have actually worked in K-12 schools). I also tell them about some of my other responsibilities in the university so they understand why I might not be in my office from 9-5 every day to answer their calls. I tell them a few things about my hobbies and my family and which college teams I root for. I believe that this personal information is important for making a connection with my students and it says to them that I am also balancing family and other responsibilities, just like many of them are.

I ask students to give me general information about themselves by filling out a note card with contact information (home and job) and their reason for taking the course.

Then on the back I ask for some personal information such as hobbies, favorite movie or TV show, etc. This allows me get to know the students and suggests ways I can draw on their experiences during class.

## The Nitty Gritty: Going Over the Syllabus

I think it is very important to go over the syllabus with the students. I particularly emphasize my contact information and highlight the quickest way to get in touch with me. Then I go on to cover class requirements and point out any unusual facts in the class schedule. I have several assignments that only make sense once the skills have been taught, so I used to only put the name of the assignment in the syllabus along with the date it was due. But this caused a lot of student anxiety, so I now have a brief description of the assignment with a estimated amount of time students will need to devote to it. Many students like to plan their workload for the semester and it really alleviated a lot of problems when I gave them a way to gauge the time needed for a particular assignment, even if they didn't totally understand what they would need to do.

## Who's Sitting Next to You: Student Introductions

I want my students to start to get to know each other in the first class. The largest number of students I ever have in a class is 30, so it is a relatively simple matter to do some kind of introduction. Because we are a commuter campus, students usually only know each other through classes. I want them to have a sense of the other students who are in the class and so I have them pair up with someone they don't know and interview each other. Then they introduce the other student. This lets people in the class see if there is someone who lives or works near them whom they might carpool with. It also gives a sense of the diversity in the class with regard

to home, jobs, hobbies, etc. If there is time, I ask the two students to see if they can find any connection between themselves (there is always something), which emphasizes the commonality among people.

## Seeing the Sizzle: Creating Interest in Content

At the end of the first class, I want students to leave with a high level of interest in the course content. If I don't always achieve that, I at least want them to leave talking about something interesting that we did that relates to the content. Sometimes it is a quick true/false test with some controversial questions. Instead of giving them the answers, I tell them they will discover the answer themselves during the course. Or I give them, "what if" case study scenarios and they turn in their answers to be checked as we get to each issue during the semester. In some required classes I do a pretest, but even though this is somewhat dull, I always try to include a few controversial questions to peak interest.

## Come Back Next Time: Ending the Class

Finally I give students a chance to ask me questions and I get some feedback from them. I usually give out a new note card and I ask them to write one or two reactions to the class, plus any questions they have. These are anonymous, unless they want me to contact them with a specific answer, but it gives me a sense of what is important to them and what they are taking away. The last thing I do is to tell them what we'll be doing at the next class with a teaser quality if possible.

## Late Registrants: Dealing with Stragglers

One of the reasons some teachers give for not doing much the first class is that there will always be some new students in the second class due to the drop/add procedures. While this is true, there are usually only a few new students so it makes little sense to lose the benefits of the first class to deal with this small minority. But to make things easier on myself, I do have a handout entitled: If you missed the first class. It has directions for the note card, lists the class rules, highlights items from the syllabus, and gives some personal information about me. This way I can just hand the sheet to students who drop by my office or who stop me outside the door as I come into the second class. Then, I meet with all the new students after the second class to see if they have any questions.

### What's in it for me: Final Thoughts

I've spent a number of semesters honing my first class activities, and I still revise what I do based on student feedback and on ideas I get at workshops. But there is also an unexpected benefit for me. By being really well prepared for the first day in class and using it to communicate my enthusiasm for the course and the students, I find that I go out of that class really excited about the semester ahead. And that attitude will have positive carryover for me and my students.

### References:

Felder, Richard. 1999. Getting started. *Chemical Engineering Education.* Vol. 29, no. 3: 166-7.

McKeachie, Wilbert J. 1994. *Teaching tips: A guide book for the beginning college teacher*, 9th ed. Lexington, Massachusetts: Heath.

Perlman, B. & McCann, L. 1999. Student perspectives on the first day of class. *Faculty Forum*, Vol. 26, no. 4.

❊ ❊ ❊

## Diffusing Course Anxiety
*Betsy Lucal*
*Sociology*
*Indiana University South Bend*

Each fall semester I teach a required course on sociological theory, a topic many students expect to be difficult. To help get a sense of how many students suffer from theory anxiety and to let students know that they are not alone in their anxiety, I ask students to complete two sentences: "Theory is…" and "The thought of studying theory makes me…" Responses to these questions help me gauge students' preconceptions (even misconceptions) about theory and to get them ready to discuss theory as a topic that they can understand after all. This discussion helps to defuse anxiety and to create a sense of camaraderie among the students. The message is that we're all in this together.

❊ ❊ ❊

## Building Rapport With Your Students
*Doug Barney*
*Business & Economics*
*Indiana University Southeast*

Why build rapport with your students? Why not just conduct the class without building rapport? After all, building rapport (creating a harmonious, and hopefully productive, connection) requires a time commitment in class and outside class, as students stop in to see you and talk and ask questions. Here are a few of the reasons you might want to build rapport with your students:

**Improved classroom performance** – While I do not have any solid statistical data and have not seen any such results anywhere, I do have students tell me that they performed better in class because I knew them and they knew I had expectations for their performance.

**That warm fuzzy feeling** – I know students by name and they ask me questions and talk with me as an individual they know and trust. This contact often continues well past completion of that course. Isn't this why we became teachers?

**Improved teaching evaluation scores** – All right, let's get down to a core issue among untenured faculty – teaching evaluations. Much literature advocates active learning and building rapport with students (although authors may not use that expression).

So how do you build rapport with your students? Here are some methods I use in my classes. Most of these methods could also be classified as approaches to active learning. Also, these approaches require me to put myself on the spot sometimes (like the first one).

**Greet your students** – I meet my students at the classroom door, sometimes on the first day of class. I may block the door and expect them to shake my hand and say hello (or something such) before they enter the room. (This can work as well at the end of class.) Now, this may not work as well if the students can enter by more than one door. I also sometimes walk around the room during class, or just before, shaking hands and talking with students. Generally students are mildly shocked by this activity the first time, and they also get some fun out of it. I sometimes joke that I am running for dogcatcher, or some likely post.

I follow up on the above activity by practicing handshakes and greetings periodically in class. When two people meet they shake hands, look at each other, and make some words of greeting. This is an important professional activity, and I expect most students will get a great benefit from it. According to Lavington (1997), "You've Only Got Three Seconds" to make the right first impression and a bad first impression takes a long time to overcome. Therefore, I practice first impressions with my students.

**Use a Seating Chart** – While this may seem old-fashioned in some ways, I find it incredibly helpful in learning students' names. I do not use it for taking attendance or for class grades. I have students write their names on a seating chart using the names they want me to call them. I then bring this chart to class and place it on the desk in the front of the room, along with my other teaching notes. As I walk around the room pulling students into the discussion, I will glance at the seating chart for a name or two of students I do not yet know. Then, when I am away from the desk I will call on these students by name. They may be surprised that I know their names and often then participate more.

**Use the Socratic Method** and call on students by name – I ask students questions that require them to think and not merely regurgitate material. This is not intended to be a pressure situation, therefore students can elect to "pass" on the question. I pause to allow time for the students to respond. This may be the hardest thing for faculty to do. Our experience has been that teaching time must be filled and that we must use all class time to cover course material. Yet, pausing gives students time to think and reflect and can reap enormous benefits. These pauses can vary from several seconds to several minutes, but I do not think I have ever paused for more than 30 seconds. By then some other student often comes to the beleaguered student's rescue.

**Tell the students about yourself**. This lets them know your background and helps them see that you can relate to them and what they are doing. I talk about my youth, education, work history, and family. Some of this talk occurs the first class day and some is scattered throughout the semester. Anecdotes used as segues between topics can enliven the class, provide humor, and build rapport.

**Strive to continuously improve** and let your students know that you make this attempt. I tell my students what I got from the periodic educational training, and practicing this training in my classes. Students are generally open to the idea of trying new things in class and forgiving when these attempts are not as successful as desired, especially if I share my plans with the class up front. For example, I recently participated in a semester-long acting class at my school, including taking part in scenes. Acting consists of individuals striving for goals and encountering obstacles, similar to the learning process in our classes. I also studied a book on "Teaching and Performing" which really helped me tie this acting experience to my teaching. Students were pleased to learn that I am also still attending classes and growing.

I firmly believe active student participation increases rapport. Besides the above activities my classrooms also include the following example active learning activities:

Students in my required core class interview with me and then interview with outside professionals, both for grades. This is a further attempt to hone their interpersonal skills and a chance for me to get to know my students better. During the interview with me my opening questions to them concern their career goals.

I ask my students typical exam questions in class, on the overhead projector. I then allow them time to work the problems and walk around the room working with students individually on the problems. As a side benefit, students who got the problem right often help students next to them who are struggling.

The above activities are a few examples of the ways I strive to develop rapport with my students. For further related reading I suggest Lavington's (1997) book, *You've Only Got Three Seconds*. Lavington will help you identify how to make a favorable first impression on your students and how you can help your students make favorable first impressions. To explore your passion for teaching try Fried's (1995)*The Passionate Teacher*. This is an exciting book devoted to helping teachers understand themselves and their roles in the classroom. If you want to encourage active learning in your classroom a good starting point for study is a book by Bonwell and Eison (1991) entitled *Active Learning: Creating Excitement in the Classroom*. This book gives some great examples for active learning activities and insights into how to make them work. I also recommend *Teaching and Performing* by Timpson, Burgoyne, Jones, and Jones (1997). This book provides a great tie between acting and teaching. The best advice I can give on building rapport, however, is the simplest: have fun and smile.

**References:**
Bonwell, Charles and James Eison. 1991. *Active learning: Creating excitement in the classroom.* New York: Wiley Publishing.

Fried, Robert.1995. *The passionate teacher.* Boston: Beacon Press.

Lavington, Camille. 1997. *You've only got t hree seconds.* New York: Doubleday Press.

Timpson, William, Suzanne Burgoyne, Christine Jones and Waldo Jones. 1997. Teaching and performing: Ideas for energizing you classes. Madison, Wisconsin: Magna Publications.

❈ ❈ ❈

## Dealing With Side Conversations

*Carol Hostetter*
*Social Work*
*Indiana University Bloomington*

Faculty often disagree about how to handle students' side conversations, yet few would disagree about the distraction it poses to faculty and students alike. Students trying to listen to the lecture and discussion *expect* the professor to do something about it. The role of the "heavy," however, appeals to few of us. I asked myself, how can I discipline the talkers and yet maintain an open and positive atmosphere in the classroom?

What I have learned to do is this. When I am lecturing and I notice a student talking, I stop, smile, and say, "That's ok, I'll wait until we're all ready." I continue to wait, smiling, until they stop (which generally occurs very soon). Then I resume without comment.

The situation is a bit different if, instead of myself speaking, a student is contributing to class discussion when the side conversation begins. When this happens, I interrupt the student who *should* have the floor by saying, "Oh, Jennifer, I'm sorry, could you wait just a minute? I'd like to wait until we're all ready." Jennifer invariably apologizes (an odd reaction, since it's not her fault), and I assure her she doesn't need to apologize, and by this time the side conversation has stopped. I say, maintaining my smile, "OK, now we're all ready, go ahead, Jennifer."

Of course, there are some students who repeatedly require intervention, in which case I catch them as they leave class and speak to them about it. For most students, however, the technique of waiting works very well. The classroom atmosphere does not become tense because I am using polite speech and a pleasant demeanor to remind the class that we are willing to wait until everyone is "on board." I believe the message students are sent (and evaluations confirm this) is that I care about their learning. I'm not willing to allow an unnecessary distraction, and students do not have the tension of being "called out." They have been sent a message without their having to lose face.

A limitation of this method is that it becomes more difficult with very large classes. Students in larger classes are better able to exhibit a lack of interest in the professor's expressions of concern. Other techniques may be more useful in large lecture halls. Whatever venue professors teach in, however, I believe they should develop some strategy for addressing the problem. If not, we give students the message that either we do not care that they are distracted, or we are powerless to do anything about it.

❈ ❈ ❈

## Getting to Know Your Students in a Large Lecture Class: Using an Online "Welcome" Message

*Kevin Glowacki*
*Classical Studies*
*Indiana University Bloomington*

Here is a "quick" strategy for getting to know students in a large lecture class by using technology to encourage early communication between student and instructor. At the beginning of each semester, I post a "welcome" message on our class website. I set this page up as a password restricted form, with the results sent to my personal email account. The very first homework assignment (actually counted as part of the class participation grade in this case) is for each student to access this page and respond to the questions there. (I usually tell the students they have one week to respond, after which I deactivate the link.). This process allows me to see that all of my students have active and properly functioning network IDs and that they know how to access the website and the various kinds of course materials I have created for them (lecture outlines, images, suggestions for further reading, study guides, etc.).

On the web page, I introduce myself and welcome them enthusiastically to the class. I then ask them to answer a few questions and share some personal information that may allow me to "customize" a portion of the class content according to their backgrounds and interests, such as...

> *Name*
> *Preferred email address*
> *Majors and minors.*
> *Previous background in this or*
> *related subjects.*
> *Reasons for choosing this class*
> *Expectations* (with some leading

questions, such as "What do you expect to learn? What do you expect to get out of the course? What do you think would make this course a success?")
*Other comments and questions they have for me.*

> **Establish an atmosphere of interaction that will carry over into the real classroom.**

Reading their responses allows me to get a good sense of the make-up and personalities of a large class within a very short period of time. I usually learn about former teachers, family vacations, books, and Discovery Channel programs that have inspired them to take my course, as well as career goals, graduation requirements, preconceptions, and performance anxieties. I learn about their diverse talents and interests and about the different approaches students take toward the learning process. Putting faces to these facts takes a good bit longer, but I feel the process is made much easier after this kind of electronic introduction since it encourages contact between student and faculty at a very early stage.

The key, for me, is to establish an atmosphere of interaction, even in a very large class, that will carry over into the real classroom. To this end, I also set up the form so that when the students submit their answers, they are automatically sent a "thank you" note and verification, along with a promise that I will respond to each of them individually via email as soon as I can. I must admit that this is a very time consuming effort during the first 2 weeks of the semester (e.g., 100 students x 5 minutes to read and respond = 500 minutes on the computer just for this class), but I think the "pay off" is well worth the effort. A simple dialogue begun online at the start of a class can easily grow into an ongoing conversation and exchange of ideas throughout the semester.

## References:

Chickering, Arthur and Stephen C. Ehrmann. 1996. Implementing the seven principles: Technology as lever. *AAHE Bulletin* (October): 3-6. Available from http://www.tltgroup.org/programs/seven.html.

❋ ❋ ❋

# The Use of Discipline Related Ice Breakers in the First Week of a Course

*Beth B. Kern*
*Business & Economics*
*Indiana University South Bend*

The first week of a course can set the tone for the entire term. Students develop expectations regarding both the instructor and the course during this time (McKeachie 1994, 21). If one wishes to foster an environment that promotes interaction among students, setting expectations during the beginning of the course is essential. Many sources offer generic suggestions for breaking the ice. (See, for example, McKeachie 1994, 22-25). While these may be quite effective in terms of facilitating student interaction at that moment, they often are not directly tied to the course subject matter.

Students often have preconceptions about certain disciplines. If the ice breakers used do not involve accounting subject matter, there is a danger that students might perceive that the field of accounting does not lend itself to interaction and communication, thereby reinforcing old stereotypes.

## Ice Breaker Example

It is possible to avoid this predicament by developing an ice breaking exercise using discipline related subject matter. The following describes a role-playing and simulation exercise as an example of an approach which both facilitates student interaction and communication while simultaneously teaching discipline specific subject matter (in this case, accounting). It can easily be incorporated in the first week of the first course in accounting and facilitates a high level of interaction among students who often do not know each other prior to attending the course.

This in-class exercise assigns students to perform roles within a set of specified transactions forming a simulation of the formation of a new business. At the beginning of class, students are asked to volunteer for the roles of banker, supplier, landlord, customer and business owner. Upon volunteering, each student indicates his or her name. That name is used throughout the exercise. For example, students will transact with "Jay the banker" at the "Bank of Jay." This assists with breaking the ice. Each volunteer is given a cupful of white poker chips. They are told that these chips represent resources. One student is assigned to each role with the exception of the owners. The number of students assigned as owners is equal to the number of firms. The number of firms is determined by forming small groups of three or four students from the remainder of the class. Each member of a business group performs a record-keeping role. Thus, each member of the class has a role in the simulation. Once the groups are formed, the students introduce themselves to each of the group members. By the end of the class, a

52

student typically knows by name at least seven members of the class.

Each business is beginning its operations. The students are asked what resources the business has at this time. It is obvious that each firm has none. They are then asked to look about the classroom. All the potential resources that a firm needs to begin a business (the white chips) are external to the firm; the firm must engage in transactions with these parties in order to procure the resources necessary to start a business.

The concept that there must be a source for every resource is discussed, and the record keeping function is then introduced. The importance of keeping track of a firm's resources, assets, as well as the sources of those resources, otherwise known as liabilities and owners' equity, is also addressed. The students then engage in transactions using the poker chips as the medium of exchange and to perform the record keeping function. Assets are represented with white poker chips, liabilities with red, and owners' equity with blue.

Several accounting concepts are introduced during the exercise. These include, but are not limited to: the accounting entity concept, revenue recognition, the matching principle, operating activities, investing activities and financing activities. These usually are not exciting concepts. Nonetheless, the role-playing simulation format fosters a lively classroom which sets the stage for the rest of the semester. Students learn not only fundamental accounting concepts but also begin to break down potential preconceptions that an accounting class, and potentially the profession itself, must be mind-numbing.

Creating discipline based ice breakers is not limited to solely role play simulations. Several active learning strategies can be used as a framework for creating an ice breaking learning experience. To function as an ice breaker, however, the experience should involve student interaction with time allotted for them to become acquainted with each other. Some possibilities include: cooperative learning exercises, debates and drama. For more information about active learning techniques, see Bonwell and Eison (1991).

**References:**
Bonwell, Charles C. and James A. Eison. 1991. Active Learning: Crating Excitement in the Classroom. *ASHE-ERIC Higher Education Report No. 1.* Washington, D.C.: George Washington University, School of Education and Human Development.

McKeachie, W. J. 1994. *Teaching Tips: Strategies, Research, and Theory for College and University Teachers,* 9th ed. Lexington, Massachusetts: D. C. Heath and Company.

❋ ❋ ❋

# Chapter 4:

# Are You Out There?

*Teachers and students together create
a community of learners.*

*Carol Hostetter*

# Communication as the Problem and the Solution

*Dorothy W. Ige*
*Communication*
*Indiana University Northwest*

Communication is the process in which senders and receivers of messages interchangeably assign meanings and interpretations to words, actions, objects and surroundings. Communication, then, is the thread that ties the fabric of the classroom teaching process together. Beginning educators receive many messages about teacher communication in the classroom, including the need to cover all units in the course, to behave firmly with students during the first few class sessions, and to know that instructing becomes easier after teaching a few times. While such advice may hold some truths, lifelong learning and thirty years of experience in teaching junior high, high school and, university students have caused me to hail other axioms: "Often, less is more," "Don't let them see you sweat," and "You cannot not communicate." Had I examined these premises with regard to teaching early in my career, I could have saved students, educational staff, and myself many headaches.

## Often, less is more

We live in a society in which we frequently hear, "More, more, more!" Do we really need a greater quantity of subject content? The quantity versus quality dichotomy is commonly played out in classrooms where a barrage of concepts are taught in a course during any given semester. The goal is to teach a plethora of contents, no matter what. Very little learning or retention takes place when concepts are hurled at students at lightning speed. Pause to ask,"Could students benefit more from really learning ten or less concepts in-depth?" For students to receive the deluge of the instructor's knowledge on the course topic in a hit-or-miss fashion is probably counterproductive to creating an atmosphere of love of lifelong learning. We know from our own experiences that we only remember a minute portion of the things to which we are exposed during a teaching or training process, and the same is true for students.

I have learned that it is best to carefully select those critical concepts that students need to learn and to focus on teaching them better with focused, calculated, and uncluttered teaching processes. Purposeful repetition of a few phenomena in various contexts on various abstract and concrete levels and analyzed from different perspectives affords students the opportunity to absorb and mentally massage the ideas in ways that can lead them to formulate and test their own hypotheses for greater understanding. If we show the relevance of lifelong learning within contexts and life experiences, we also communicate to students what is really important.

## Don't let them see you sweat

It is okay to sweat, but students, parents, and school officials need not witness our being petrified. Adrenalin rushes for the first day of teaching are natural and understandable. Nothing increases confidence more than being prepared. As teachers, we owe it to ourselves and to our students to master the art and skill of the subject to be taught.

Beyond being prepared, we need the courage to challenge ourselves as educators and to challenge our students. We may make mistakes. That is okay. Discovery is born of experimentation. Exercises, group work and other techniques may prove challenging for teachers who have taught in traditionally structured ways, such as lecturing to passive students. Reasonable experimentation can create alternative ways of knowing and generate new knowledge for the future. Thus, sensible risk-taking stretches the teacher and the learner. This does not mean that teaching is a creative, unfocused laissez-faire operation with students failing to make the connection between simulations, role plays, or other engaging activities and the salient course materials. As a former junior high and high school drama and speech teacher, it became apparent to me that, even in performance units, more structured syllabi "maps" of the courses with clear objectives and aligned class agendas that could be used in flexible ways would be as helpful for me as to the students in directing their experiential learning. Knowing how to choose tools to evaluate objective and subjective class work helps students and the teacher feel better about the reliability of the assessment of their work.

While teacher mastery of the subject matter is assumed for effective teaching, the image that the teacher knows all is one of bondage for both instructor and learner. Still, if a question is asked to which the teacher does not know the answer, saying so and promising and following through on getting the answer to the learner shows that both the teacher and the student are engaged, lifelong learners.

If preparation time and organization are essential to effective teaching, so is taking care of oneself physically. The "less is more" concept works here, too. Handling one's stress through less caffeine, more physical activity, more sleep and fewer negative thoughts affects classroom communication and teaching success. Positive behaviors often give rise to positive internal messages and health that result in positive verbal and nonverbal messages that radiate out to others.

**You cannot not communicate**

It is very difficult to not participate in self-communication or assign meaning to the verbal and nonverbal behavior of self and others. As a beginning teacher, I wish someone had told me to pay more attention to both student interpersonal communication and to communication with the school's administrative staff.

For students, effective interpersonal skills can be as important as the subject matter content. I found it is best to use my own teaching style rather than trying to use someone else's mode of instruction. Students can easily recognize that which is genuine. It is crucial to remember to be fair to all and to recognize the diversity of students and the diversity of learning styles.

I wish I had understood the importance of appropriately compassionate, open-minded, collegial interactions with peers, administrators, and all of those who are involved in the educational milieu of the institution. In dealing with administration, you must know what is important to them and make it important to you. Deans, principals, and department chairs often cannot afford the narrow view of the classroom only, but must focus holistically on the macrocosm of the educational process. There are classroom goals, but there are also institution and community goals that affect the educational process at every level, including classroom and student outcomes. Being clear on the academic hierarchy and understanding how to use the system to appropriately request what is needed to effect the teacher's own

> **Very little learning or retention takes place when concepts are hurled at students at lightning speed.**

58

learning and that of students (equipment, space, start-up costs, software, more grant and travel funds for development, etc.), are crucial elements. Being an ethical team player goes a long way with everyone—including the administrative staff, custodian and secretary. The janitor will often find the long extension cord you requested, when supposedly none existed, if you have treated him or her with respect. Every institution has its own culture—some are informal "work hard, play hard" and others are formal "work hard, work hard" environments. It is wise to be cognizant of the organizational climate. Student-centeredness is the commonality that should bridge all facets of the educational arena.

In essence, if we focus on quality rather than quantity of teaching content, and prepare carefully, deliberately, and flexibly in ways that cause less stress to learners and ourselves, we can use our verbal and nonverbal skills to positively affect our own learning, as well as that of students. Communication inside and outside the classroom is key. It can be a problem, but it can also be a solution. Happy teaching.

※ ※ ※

## Getting Students to Talk – From Day One
*Betsy Lucal*
*Sociology*
*Indiana University South Bend*

After a semester spent teaching a classroom full of students who tended to just look at me when I asked a question or requested their input, I realized that getting students to talk on the first day of class made discussion throughout the term much easier. At the very least, this signals to students that my questions are not rhetorical and that I am serious about wanting classroom

discussion. In each of my courses, I have a first-day exercise that requires or at least encourages many students to participate in the discussion. In my sociology of gender course, I ask each student to name something that we use to tell men and women apart. The list they generate becomes the basis for our first discussion. In introduction to sociology, I ask the class three questions: What do you expect to happen in class today? How do you know I'm the professor? What makes you think I might not be the professor after all? (The third questions is added to the list on the board after students have had time to answer the first two questions.) Student responses to these questions provide me an opportunity for talking about the variety of sociological topics we will cover in the course.

※ ※ ※

## Facilitating Daily Classroom Conversations: Pedagogy in Action
*Stuart Schrader*
*Indiana University-Purdue University Indianapolis*

In my teaching, I borrow from some of the learning philosophy and techniques embedded in problem-based learning (PBL). A PBL approach emphasizes that knowing is continually changing (MacDonald and Issacs 2001). Throughout the process "the faculty facilitates the development of the student's reasoning process, guiding them [only] when necessary, and challenging the depth…of understanding and application of concepts" (Williams 2001, 87). The teacher in this process guides, but as Dewey (1938) suggests, does not interfere or control student learning. Students in this process work in small groups through peer teaching in order to help each other connect new and prior understandings (Williams 2001). By exploring connections between practical situations and conceptual processes, students are continuously restructuring their knowledge as they work toward their best outcome (Williams 2001).

In my courses, I have adopted a problem-based learning style in which students are encouraged to participate in a process of free inquiry that systematically helps them as a group to develop through a series of critical inquiries. In order to search for the best possible outcome, "through collaboration with classmates, students refine and enhance their [understandings] and skills. [Further], when possible outcomes have been identified, students present, justify, and debate each possibility" (Williams 2001, 90).

Below is the model I use for discussions in Communication Theory:

The following daily routine is designed to assist the class in developing a relationally responsible learning community that fosters the practice of life-long learning. Students are asked to actively engage in an educational environment that facilitates the teacher as student and student as teacher.

I. **Announcements**

II. **Learning Issue Questions**
(6-7 member groups)
A. Prior to Class
Each person needs to write one question they have about their readings and a brief (2-3 sentences) yet complete response that attempts to answer that question. Place that question and response onto Oncourse under the appropriate discussion header before the reading is due in class.

B. In Class
1. Hand your question to another person to read in your group.
2. Then have each member of the group read a learning issue question out loud.
3. Have the group decide which ONE learning issue the group would like to discuss with the class.
4. Have one person read the question to the class. On days when we have two chapters (theories) to discuss, we may only select 2 or 3 people to raise their learning issues per theory.
5. After the class has discussed the learning issue (question), then please read your answer.

III. **Critical Analysis**
A. Prior to Class
One person selected from each group should write one paragraph critiquing the theory (theories) for that day. Please use Griffen's criteria for Interpretive vs. Objective in order to determine if the theory is more appropriately described as interpretive or objective and why. How successfully does it meet the appropriate criteria set forth by Griffen?
B. In Class
1. The selected person from the group is asked to read aloud their paragraph to their group.
2. The group should reflect on their remarks and ask any necessary clarification questions.
3. Then selected people from various groups will be asked to share with the class

at large their critique.

4. The class should reflect upon the questions and/or issues raised by the critical analysis paragraph.

## V. Praxis Reflection

### A. Prior to Class

One person selected from each group should write one paragraph to explain how the chapter's ideas (concepts) being discussed for that day can be put into practice in one's personal and/or professional everyday life.

### B. In Class

1. The selected person from the group is asked to read aloud their paragraph to their group.

2. The group should reflect on their remarks and ask any necessary clarification questions.

3. Then selected people from various groups will be asked to share with the class at large their critique.

4. The class should reflect upon the questions and/or issues raised by the praxis reflection.

## In-class Process

1. Break immediately into Groups; begin discussion about theory

2. Announcements

3. Reflect on comments from the last group meeting (select a scribe/ spokesperson for this upcoming session).

4. Have the group discuss all of the following in sequence:

a. Select ONE learning issue question to discuss per theory (if there are two theories for the day, then discuss two learning issues unless otherwise instructed.)

b. Discuss a critical analysis for each theory (if there are two theories for the day, then discuss two critiques unless otherwise instructed.)

c. Discuss a praxis paragraph for each theory (if there are two theories for the day, then discuss two praxis statements unless otherwise instructed.)

5. Discuss items in the following order with the entire class:

a. Learning Issue Question (per theory)

b. Critical Analysis (per theory)

c. Praxis (per theory)

Note: When exploring theories consider the following:

1. Are theories value laden?

a. Can they be right or wrong?

b. Can a theory be helpful or harmful? How so?

2. Is the theory more like a map or a story or both?

Note: The aforementioned schedule maybe altered at various times to allow for activities, exercises, video clips and experiential learning experiences.

## References:

Dewey, John. 1938. *Experience and education.* New York: Macmillian.

MacDonald, D. and G. Issacs. 2001. Developing a professional identity through problem based learning. *Teaching Education* 12, no. 3: 315-333.

Williams, Bev. 2001. The theoretical links between problem-based learning and self directed learning for continuing professional nursing education. *Teaching in Higher Education* 6, no. 1: 85-98.

✳ ✳ ✳

## What Do Your Students Really Know?

*Charles R. Barman*
*School of Education*
*Indiana University-Purdue University Indianapolis*

As a new faculty member several years ago, I remember being excited to share all the information I had gained with my students. Because my introductory science students had experienced at least one laboratory science course in high school, I assumed that they had a good grasp of most basic science concepts. Not long into my teaching career, this assumption was shattered.

### A True Story

Before plunging into the topic of gravity, I decided to ask my students a few questions and do a simple demonstration. I stood at the front of my class of thirty students and held in each hand a different size ball of clay. (One ball was obviously larger and more massive than the other.) Both balls were held at the same distance from the floor. I looked directly at my students and asked: If I drop these two balls of clay at the same time, will they hit the floor at the same time, or will one reach the floor first? To my amazement, about half of my class thought the larger ball would hit the floor first and most of the remaining students in class were unsure. A few students used terminology, such as acceleration and force, but were unable to provide a reasonable explanation of what would happen when the balls were dropped to the floor. Then, when I proceeded to drop the two balls, many of the students confirmed their original misconception by declaring the larger ball hit the floor first. In other words, these students made inaccurate observations to fit their current views about gravity. It is hard to determine how these students arrived at their ideas about gravity. Perhaps they had observed a rock and a leaf fall to the ground. Without being able to identify all relevant variables related to this phenomenon, such as air resistance, it would be easy to conclude that the gravitational effect on heavier objects is greater than on lighter ones. However, regardless of the way in which they arrived at their conclusions, I was faced with the realization that before any significant progress could be made about the concept of gravity, it would be imperative to help these students question their thinking about this basic science topic.

### Vital Information Related to Teaching

The "gravity story" is a textbook example of what many educators refer to as student misconceptions or naive concepts (Osborne and Freyberg 1985). The study of student misconceptions has been an important area of educational research (Novak, 1987). Basically, the findings from this research conclude that students enter our classrooms with preconceived ideas about the natural world. These ideas may or may not be consistent with the accepted views of the specific academic discipline. If their initial ideas are incorrect and are not challenged, they will continue to hold on to these concepts throughout their lives (Bransford, Brown, and Cocking 2000). In addition, students will incorporate new information into their original ideas in

> **Students enter our classrooms with preconceived ideas.**

an attempt to hold on to their preconceptions. As Driver (1983) describes, the teacher's task is to encourage students to re-check their observations and perhaps compare them with one another until everyone is in agreement. The teacher needs to help students sort out relevant from irrelevant data and, in some cases, where direct observations may not be enough to fully represent a specific phenomenon, the teacher may need to use direct instruction to assist in clarification.

It is also very important to understand that students may use correct terminology when asked a question about a specific subject, making the student appear like he or she understands what is being addressed. Or, they may also be able to circle the "correct" term or word on a test. However, this does not indicate whether they truly understand the complexities of the subject. It only means that they were able to memorize or recognize certain terminology (Bransford, Brown, and Cocking 2000). To find out a student's complete understanding, one must ask appropriate questions related to a concept and require the student to provide a complete explanation of the concept.

### My Advice
So, my advice to a new faculty member would be, don't automatically make assumptions about your students' understanding of basic concepts related to your academic discipline. Remember, that students have a difficult time letting go of their original concepts. And, when addressing a new topic, think of ways to find out what your students already know about this topic. Then, begin your presentation of the topic at the level of your students' understanding.

### References:
Bransford, John D., Ann L. Brown, and Rodney R. Cocking, eds. 2000. *How people learn: Brain, mind, experience, and school*. Washington D.C.: National Academy Press.

Driver, Rosalind. 1983. *The pupil as scientist?* Milton Keynes, England: The Open University Press.

Novak, Joseph Donald. 1987. *Proceedings of the second international seminar on misconceptions and educational strategies in science and mathematics, July 26-29, 1987, Cornell University, Ithaca, NY, USA*. New York: Cornell University.

Osborne, Roger and P. S. Freyberg. 1985. *Learning in science: The implications of children's science*. Auckland, New Zealand: Heinemann.

❊ ❊ ❊

## Community of Learners
*Carol Hostetter*
*Social Work*
*Bloomington*

If you believe, as I do, that teachers and students together create a community of learners, and that each person both contributes to and is affected by our shared culture, then you may be interested in making this sometimes invisible process more visible. With the help of other students and faculty in our small program, I developed a tool that provides the means for metacommunicating about our community of learners and assessing it (us).

All third-year students in the School of Social Work take the same four courses, and repeat the process in the spring with four new courses. They suddenly must write more, apply the concepts more, and work in group projects more than they have ever done. They spend a great deal of time with each other and the faculty over the course of the year. I refer to it as the "all social work, all the time" channel. It's an intense experience in which the demands are balanced by the rewards of the changes we see in May. Many difficulties arise from the challenging academic content, but perhaps more spring from the interpersonal processes among students.

In order to help guide students through this personal and academic marathon, the faculty take the first day of class to orient students to us and to each other. We conduct an activity called "The Community of Learners." Students form small groups, each with one faculty member, and discuss their hopes and fears for the coming school year. Each group develops a list of positive behaviors students expect from faculty and peers. The groups recombine, remove duplicates, clarify differences, and develop a final list. The list is sorted into sections, typed and distributed to students shortly after. The sections developed generally include expectations for faculty, expectations for students in general, and expectations for students in group projects.

Interestingly, students set high standards for their own classroom conduct, for example, expecting each other to come to classes prepared, be respectful of personal boundaries, and maintain civil behavior. In group projects, students want others to attend meetings promptly, communicate if they cannot attend, share the work, and find each others' strengths and talents. Students want faculty to provide support for student learning through creating a comfortable classroom atmosphere, integrating the readings into class discussion, and treating students as adults. While these are only a few examples of the expectations, they show the

value of having students generate their own criteria.

The list is then used to create a survey tool, given periodically throughout the school year. The tool is valuable for both acquiring quantitative information and for providing an opportunity for class discussion on "how are we doing?" With this level of power and accountability, the "we" clearly feels like a group of individuals, connected by a bond: our community of learners.

❋ ❋ ❋

## Arranging the Room: Promoting Student Interaction

*Pat Ashton*
*Sociology*
*Indiana University Purdue-University Fort Wayne*

I once sat in on a small seminar course at an elite liberal arts college. The instructor was highly knowledgeable and extremely enthusiastic about the subject matter. She emphasized that discussion among class members was a vital part of the course. Yet, when I looked around, I saw that the desks were arranged in four neat rows facing the teacher's desk at the front of the room! The intelligent, highly motivated students enrolled in the course managed to have lively discussions anyway. But I was struck by the fact that generally the design of space does matter! If you emphasize discussion in your course, consider arranging the students' desks in a circle or a horseshoe. It changes the whole dynamic of a room when students can actually look at one another, instead of at the back of one another's heads. Even in a predominantly lecture-oriented class, it may make sense to alter the seating arrangement. If we don't believe that we as the instructor are the "sage on the stage," then why arrange the room to give that cue? My Introductory

Sociology course, like many intro courses, is predominantly lecture-oriented with an enrollment of 40+. Given space limitations in the classroom, I have to have students in a horseshoe 2 rows deep around the room. But this means that no student is more than 2 rows from the front, and all of the students can see each other. This arrangement has increased the amount of discussion in the classroom and made the interchange between the students and me more conversational and intimate. Term after term, the students rate this feature highly on the course evaluations and have many positive comments. Some instructors who follow me into the classroom have experienced the alternative arrangement when my students forgot to rearrange the desks after class. A number of those instructors have now started asking me to leave the desks in the horseshoe shape! Imagine if this was to become the norm for arranging desks in a classroom and those who wanted them in straight rows facing the front would be the ones who had to rearrange the room before each class!

**Classroom Management Techniques: Direct Communication**

Most instructors have had little training in handling conflict or disruptive behaviors in the classroom. When confronted with these problems, we are often tempted to hide behind the façade of our authority. While threats and power may work in the short run, in the long run they are counterproductive as they alienate many students and wind up actually undermining the instructor's authority and credibility. Consider the situation where two students are whispering back and forth during a lecture and clearly annoying the lecturer. We've all had it happen to us. Most times, we glance over at them, hoping that that will be enough to make them stop. If they don't, we escalate our dirty looks in their direction. As the rest of the class becomes aware that

we are annoyed, tension builds. Insights from the lecture are lost as attention is increasingly focused on the unfolding drama. A few students may be hoping for a dramatic confrontation, but most are increasingly uneasy. If things continue to escalate to the point where you the instructor explode, you are highly likely to resort to some sort of threat or power trip. While the immediate problem of the talking is solved, a bitter taste is created and the classroom atmosphere is spoiled.

A better way to handle this is through direct communication, or "I messages." I messages provide information to others about *my* emotions, *my* needs and preferences, *my* intentions or purposes, and/or the impact of their actions on *me*. A proper I message is about specific events or actions and it avoids blaming or accusing others. We cannot really know what other people are thinking, nor what their motivation is. When we make assumptions about their thinking, we risk being wrong and, what is worse, escalating the conflict. So, when the talking students disrupt our lecture, we might stop and say, in a calm and non-accusatory way, "I am finding it hard to lecture when you are talking too. I would prefer that you wait until after class to confer among yourselves." Notice that there is no accusation here, and no attempt to make the have the students lose face. You have focused on the problem behavior, and not made the students' character or commitment or integrity the issue. When you use this technique, you may be pleasantly surprised at what happens next. Often the guilty students will quickly apologize, which they feel comfortable doing since you haven't caused them to lose personal face (though they may be embarrassed). Or you may have created an opening for students to explain their behavior, which you may find, much to your surprise, was not at all what you perceived it to be. For example: "Sorry, Professor, but Student X told me that she had fainted earlier, and she was looking pretty pale so I was just checking with her to make sure she was okay." This was probably not what we assumed was happening at all. But now we have opened the door to sharing information.

Remember, the key to direct communication is not to threaten ("You had better, or else…."), judge ("That was really stupid."), accuse ("What's wrong with you? What were you thinking?"), or preach ("You ought to know better than that."). By taking responsibility for our own feelings and actions, we encourage students to do the same and thereby help to build an atmosphere of mutual respect in the classroom.

### In the classroom and in our offices: Dealing with angry students and colleagues

Anger is a universal human emotion. Although it takes many forms – fretting, annoyance, irritability, rage – anger is rooted in other emotions: fear, insecurity, helplessness or loss of control, a sense of being personally devalued or disrespected. Anger is basically an assertion of self. It says, "Hey, listen to me!" It is important to remember that angry behavior is a choice. People and events don't make us angry; they trigger perceptions that we use to make ourselves angry. An angry person can be frightening and upsetting. Of course they may be deliberately using anger as a weapon to unsettle you. Or they may be entirely caught up in their own feelings of being hurt, wronged, or disrespected. When a person expresses strong anger or hostility toward you, here are some ways you can de-escalate the level of emotion.

**Don't tell an angry person to calm down!** This is worst thing you can do – it is equivalent to pouring gasoline on a fire! An angry person thinks they have been wronged and that they have a right to be angry. Denying them this perceived right will only make them more angry.

**Stay calm and listen.** Rising to meet their anger will only escalate the situation. Remember that anger is contagious – and so is calm. Don't try to explain or defend yourself, or point out where the angry person is mistaken. Take some deep breaths and try to relax and focus. Listen carefully to what they are saying, and speak in a voice significantly quieter than the angry person.

**Paraphrase.** Paraphrasing – restating the message someone is communicating and reflecting the emotions they are conveying – is the most effective thing you can do with an intensely angry person. First of all, it lets them know that you are hearing their concerns. Being heard deflates their "emotional balloon" and de-escalates the anger. An angry person feels justified in their anger. When their reasons for being angry are heard, it removes much of the emotional need to be angry. Second, when you are paraphrasing, the angry person's story is the only thing being discussed, and it is extremely difficult for someone to argue with their own story. Third, the process of active listening – while it should not be deliberately designed to do so – actually slows the angry person down. This de-escalates their anger, as it is difficult to maintain an intense emotional state for long. Finally, the process of restating and reflecting forces the angry person to actually hear what they are saying, and they may decide that they are overreacting.

**Validate the angry person's feelings.** Validation does not mean agreement with the angry person's point of view, reasoning, or specific arguments. It simply means acknowledging that you understand that they are angry, and why they are angry.

**Try to reframe the issue in more neutral terms** . Keep the focus on the problem. Ignore personal attacks and provocations if at all possible. People can't fundamentally change who they are, but they can change their behavior. Focus on the parts of the problem that can be changed.

**Point out new information.** Anger is often generated by misunderstandings. When you point out information that you are hearing for the first time, you acknowledge a problem without making it personal. You also provide a way for the angry person to save face.

**Don't respond until the other person is ready to hear you.** Wait until you have significantly deflated the angry person's emotional balloon. If the person resorts to an angry position again, resume your active listening.

❋ ❋ ❋

## "Are There Any Questions?"
*Iztok Hozo*
*Mathematics*
*Indiana University Northwest*

Something I always tell my Math for Teachers classes is that a typical student will take at least 20 - 30 seconds to formulate a response to a "harder question" and gather courage to actually raise her or his hand. By a "harder question", I mean a question for which a student hasn't heard or read the answer before and has to think about it. I tell my future teachers, let's count out 30 seconds (silently), and they are always amazed how long 30 seconds seems in the classroom. That is also the least amount of time we should give our students after asking "Are there any questions?"

❋ ❋ ❋

## How Do You Know What Your Students Know?
## Determining Student Prior Knowledge Using Web-based Warm Up Exercises
*Kathleen A. Marrs*
*Department of Biology*
*Indiana University Purdue University Indianapolis*

As a new instructor, I once gave a carefully planned and skillfully executed (I thought!) lecture on two major concepts in Biology, photosynthesis and respiration. I was dismayed to find out, after taking questions from students after the lecture, that I had completely over-estimated the student's knowledge of basic chemistry that I had assumed they should have had as a starting point for that evening's class. Students revealed numerous misconceptions in their questions after class and showed a great deal of confusion about material that I could have easily addressed earlier in that evening's lecture, had I been aware that they were unfamiliar with much of the material I assumed they already knew.

Knowing what students already know before coming to your class is an important tool in helping students to learn new material. Extensive research has shown that students learn best by a learning process termed "constructivism", which involves actively constructing new knowledge from the prior knowledge, information and experiences that students bring to class. Constructivism is one of the most well-supported theories of human learning in the research literature (Bybee; Bransford; Leonard). We know from constructivist learning theory that without identifying and activating students' prior knowledge, it is difficult for new learning to take place (Bybee; Bransford). How can a faculty member uncover and identify prior knowledge and use this to help students learn new knowledge?

---

**Knowing what students already know...is an important tool in helping students to learn.**

---

In my classes, I use the Internet as a tool to determine students' prior knowledge by assigning pre-class Warm Up assignments. These assignments are a key part of Just-in-Time Teaching (JiTT), a pedagogical strategy developed at IUPUI that has been shown to promote active learning and promote student learning (Marrs and Blake; Marrs and Novak; Novak). Each Friday, I post one or two Warm Up assignments to my course web page, along with the textbook readings and lecture outlines for the following week's classes. Each Warm Up assignment has at least 3 questions that relate to the coming week's subject material.

A Warm Up assignment is NOT a pre-lecture quiz about factual knowledge found in the text, but instead asks students to address open-ended questions that require them to think about the material that will be discussed in class and answer in their own words. Some examples for starting Warm Up questions include:

"What is the difference between...?"
"Why do you think...?"
"What determines ....?"
"What happens if...?"
"Do you think that...?"
"Estimate how many..."
"In your **own** words, explain..." (especially good for translating chemical reactions, mathematical equations into real words!)
"Explain your choice."--always a good ending for a Warm Up question!

Examples of Warm Up questions I use in my classes include: "What is the difference between a theory and a belief? " before a unit on evolution, or "Why do you think chemotherapy drugs make a person's hair fall out?" before a unit on mitosis. Students do the assigned readings before answering the Warm Ups, and answer the questions on-line through the course web pages, submitting their answers to me at least 2 hours before class time. Students typically reveal, through their Warm Up answers, ideas based on not only their prior knowledge of the subject (from high school, other college courses, or the media) but also new information from reading the textbook (Marrs and Blake; Novak).

I collect students' responses from the web file where they are stored and look through them before class. Based on student responses, I determine where to adjust the upcoming classroom lesson "Just-in-Time" for class, and show examples of students' responses in class (identified by an anonymous nickname) to confront and dispel misconceptions during class time (Marrs and Blake; Marrs and Novak; Novak). Students therefore participate in a class that is based on their prior knowledge, as a foundation on which to construct further knowledge of the subject matter.

Students' answers do not have to be complete, or even correct. In fact, we have found that partially correct responses are the most useful to determine student beliefs, prior knowledge, and misconceptions (Marrs and Blake; Novak). To ease the pressure of submitting an answer that may be incomplete or just plain incorrect, full points are given to all students who respond on time (3 points per Warm Up assignment per week, about 8% of the total points for the class). Warm Up responses are not graded as right or wrong since the material has not yet been discussed in class, but are instead used as a formative assessment tool to reveal students' prior knowledge before class time.

Assessment results of using JiTT and Warm Up assignments on student learning have been positive, with Warm Up assignments increasing the number of students who come to class prepared, and who successfully pass the course. In addition, students report that Warm Up assignments decrease the need for students to 'cram' for exams (Marrs and Blake; Marrs and Novak). Student satisfaction with JiTT is very high, with a vast majority of students stating in their end-of-course evaluations that they would prefer that most of their classes be taught in this format!

As a faculty member, I find that knowing what my students know before class is one of the most valuable tools I have to help students construct new knowledge, develop a deep understanding of the course material, and become engaged, interactive learners.

**References:**

Bybee Roger W., ed. 2002. *Learning science and the science of learning.* ArlingtonVirginia: National Science Teachers Association.

Bransford, John D., Ann L.Brown, and Rodney R. Cocking. 2000. *How people learn: Brain, mind, experience and school.* Washington D.C.: National Academy Press; available from http://books.nap.edu books/0309070368/html/index.html. Accessed 1 July 2003.

Gavrin, Andrew A., Kathleen A. Marrs, Robert E. Blake, Jeffrey X. Watt. n.d. WebScience at IUPUI. Indianapolis: IndianaUniversity-Purdue University Indianapolis; available from http://webphysics.iupui.edu/ webscience/webscience.html. Accessed 18 August 2003.

Leonard, William H. 1997 How do College Students Learn Science? In *Methods of effective teaching and course management for university and college science teachers*, ed. by Eleanor D. Siebert, Mario W. Caprio, Carri M. Lyda. Dubuque Iowa: Kendall-Hunt Publishers.

Marrs, Kathleen A. *Biology 540 -- Topics in Biotechnology. 2003.* Indianapolis: Indiana University-Purdue University Indianapolis, Department of Biology; available at http:/www.biology.iupui.edu/ biocourses/Biol540/. Accessed 18 August 2003.

Marrs, Kathleen A. 2003. *Biology N100: Contemporary Biology, Winter / Spring 2003.* Indianapolis: Indiana University-Purdue University Indianapolis, Department of Biology; available from http: //www.biology.iupui.edu/biocourses/N100/. Accessed 18 August 2003.

Marrs Kathleen A., Robert E. Blake, and Andrew.D Gavrin. 2003. Use of Warm up exercises injust in time teaching: Determining students' prior knowledge and misconceptions in biology, chemistry, and physics. *(Journal of College Science Teaching*, forthcoming).

Marrs, Kathleen A. and G. Novak. 2003. Just-in-time teaching in biology: Creating an active learner classroom using the internet. *(Cell Biology Education*, forthcoming).

Novak, G. 2003. *Just-in-time teaching.* Indianapolis: Indiana University-Purdue University Indianapolis; available from http://webphysics.iupui.edu/jitt/jitt.html. Accessed August 2003.

Novak, Gregor M., E. T. Patterson, Andrew D. Gavrin, and W. Christian. 1999. *Just-in-time teaching: Blending active learning with web technology.* Upper Saddle River, New Jersey: Prentice Hall.

✳ ✳ ✳

## Life Happens
*S. Holly Stocking*
*Journalism*
*Indiana University Bloomington*

It took me a long time to realize that if some students don't learn, it may not be my fault. Students have lives. They dive into experiences in ways that steal time from

| Students have lives. |

the books. They fall in and out of love. They help friends in crisis. Some just stay up all night talking, or run outside in the middle of the night to watch a meteor shower and sleep through the morning's alarm. Life happens. I wish I had understood that as a new teacher,

and hadn't taken the lapses in learning so personally. We all do the best we can, and sometimes life interrupts the best-laid plans.

✳ ✳ ✳

## The Student Panel as a Class-Participation Technique
*Rick Aniskiewicz*
*Sociology*
*Indiana University Kokomo*

### The Pedagogical Issue

Many instructors in introductory level and advanced courses face the somewhat challenging task of soliciting and sustaining class-participation in the form of questions, presentations, and discussions. One can attempt to initiate participation via both informal and formal mechanisms. Informal mechanisms rely on the students to spontaneously engage themselves with the material by raising questions and issues within the context of a class session. Formal mechanisms attempt to schedule and/or "structure such participation in advance by alerting the students to the fact that they will be required to discuss/present/collaborate, etc at specific points in the semester. Participation generated by informal mechanisms is often of very high-quality and enthusiasm, perhaps because it is given freely. On the downside, however, is the very real possibility that students will not want to give anything freely, thus creating those awkward pauses when nothing is said, and who among us has not been there! On the other hand, participation generated by formal (scheduled/structured) mechanisms can be quite rich and engaging, thus providing a good experience for both students and faculty. I have had success in terms of using student-panels as a formal class-participation technique.

## The Course Context

I use student panels in my S101 Social Problems and Policies course. The course has a maximum enrollment of 45 but typically enrolls between 25-35 students. This lower-level course is taken by students who run the gamut in terms of background characteristics dealing with class standing, ability/motivation, GPA, etc. Therefore, each class seems to have its own chemistry (a particular mix of students) that cannot be discerned in advance. Or, to paraphrase Forest Gump, in this class "you never know what you're gonna get".

## Student Panels: A Description

Panels refer to between 4 and 7 students who are given three questions that they need to answer in writing and that they need to present orally in class. The questions are given a week in advance of the panel-date and students do not have to rehearse and/or share their answers with the other members of the panel. Students who are not a part of a given panel constitute the audience and they are invited to respond to the panel members with their own observations. All students--not just the panel members--must turn in written answers to the panel questions after the class session. The instructor functions as a moderator/discussant. More specifically, the instructor is engaged with the technique by ensuring that all panel members have sufficient time to offer answers, ensuring that the audience has sufficient time to join the discussion, and that the tone/content of the discussion follows general standards for decorum appropriate for a college classroom. There are between 4 and 6 panels per-course and, once again, this is determined by the overall course enrollment. Thus, the technique ensures that all students will be on one panel and will be members of the audience an additional 3 to 5 times.

## Panel Questions: Some Examples

Most recently the course consisted of five panels dealing with the following topics: work/corporate power; health care; crime/criminal justice; poverty; gender and society. Students can use the chapters in the text that cover these topics as background material, but the questions (and answers) transcend anything that can be found in the text. More specifically, good panel questions animate students to think and reflect. On the other hand, bad panel questions would be those for which one could find the answer in the book. Each topic is associated with three questions and the questions vary in terms of the cognitive abilities and substantive understanding that the instructor hopes to bring to the surface. All questions attempt to facilitate at least some critical thinking ability (i.e., evidence that the students see the complexity of an issue and that they can grasp contrasting points of view). I have employed three different types of questions in an effort to engage the students and to facilitate critical thinking. These are: questions that attempt to develop a connection between the "personal" and the "social"; questions that aim to solicit student opinion; questions that attempt to get students to think about policy issues. There is, of course, some overlap between the questions (or, specific questions might include connections, opinions, or policies) although the questions vary in terms of their emphasis. Examples follow:

**A personal/social connection question.** Topic: work/corporate power. The authors give considerable attention to work and work related problems. Consider (reflect upon) your own career goals. Specifically, what are your career-goals? In other words, what would you like to achieve with your education after you graduate from college? What are the factors that have shaped (influenced) your career goals.

Finally, what obstacles can you anticipate in terms of achieving your goals?

**An opinion question.**
Topic: Gender and Society. What does the word Afeminism@ mean to you? Also, what do you feel the feminist movement has achieved and is attempting to achieve?

**A policy question.**
Topic: Crime/Criminal Justice. What is your understanding of the relationship between guns, gangs, and violence? Also, what types of policies should this country follow in terms of violence in general and guns/gangs in particular?

**Observations/Suggestions**
I have used panels in my lower level course on Social Problems and Policies for several years and have been very satisfied with this technique in terms of the goals set for student engagement and participation. The technique has not been used in a class with over 45 students and, as such, I don't know if it would succeed in larger classes, given the scheduling logistics (ensuring enough panels) and time constraints (ensuring that the instructor has sufficient time to cover content from the chapters themselves). The technique presupposes that students have at least a general interest in--and often engagement with--the material.

Thus, the panel technique seeks to identify and nurture such interest. Instructors are encouraged to NOT begin by assuming that students don't want to talk and/or that they don't want to participate. These assumptions could simply lead to a self-fulfilling prophecy. Also, be aware that students will sometimes provide answers that involve their own personal experiences with issues like divorce, family violence, discrimination/sexism, and tracking in school. The role of the instructor in these instances is to see to it that the responses

are used to illustrate specific sociological topics/problems/ concepts, etc. I have found that my own role as a moderator/discussant has evolved and improved over the years in terms of my ability to raise follow-up questions and to complete the panels in the time allotted for the class (75 minutes), but this just illustrates that teaching gets better with practice.

Good luck to all who might want to use this technique, and please feel free to contact me if I can embellish any of the points raised and/or if you have questions.

✳ ✳ ✳

## How Do I Know What They Know?
*Kevin Sue Bailey*
*Education*
*Indiana University Southeast*

Traffic, parking, walking in the freezing cold, greeting friends, and tripping over the

> **Our job is to refocus [students'] thoughts on our course content.**

chair that wasn't there yesterday…Dozens of events and thoughts occupy our students' minds as they tumble into class each day. Our job is to refocus those thoughts on our course content. Beginning class with a reconnection activity allows us to focus the brain on the here and now, check for understanding, and segue into the day's lesson. "Quick Writes" or "Admit Slips" get the job done expediently. As students enter class have a writing prompt posted on the board or screen. The prompt might ask the following:
> *What is your understanding of the concepts that we discussed yesterday?*
> *What three big ideas have stuck with you since we were together last?*

72

*What questions are still lingering in your head about yesterday's topic?*
*What is clear and what is hazy from your reading assignment (or last class)?*

Once students have written a personal response, invite them to turn to the person next to them and share their thoughts (5 minutes). Call time and ask for volunteers to share their understandings or concerns. This is a good time to verify that students understand the content covered thus far and to clarify any contradictory information that the students may have realized in their partner conversations.

Checking for understanding is an obvious benefit for this strategy. In addition, the procedure as described is in keeping with the research on brain-compatible learning. Putting our thoughts in writing triggers the brain to process information more deeply. Likewise, Kay Burke with Skylight Publications refers to the partner discussion as "oral rehearsal" and Pat Wolfe terms this process as "elaborative rehearsal." In this portion of the procedure, students must process their thinking in order to say out loud what their understanding is. This part of the lesson engages students as active participants in the class and puts every voice into the room. Instructors benefit from this short introduction to class because it allows them to quickly assess their starting point for the day, and the procedure provides a smooth transition into the next lesson. Such a simple start to class can provide both the teacher and the learner with a more successful classroom experience.

## References:

Caine, Geoffrey, Renate Nummela Caine, and Sam Crowell. 1999. *Mindshifts: A brain-compatible process for professional development and the renewal of education*, 2ded. Tuscon, Arizona: Zephyr Press.

Garmston, Robert. 1997. *The Presenter's fieldbook: A practical guide.* Norwood, Massachusetts: Christopher-Gordon Publishers Inc.

Jensen, Eric. 1998. *Introduction to brain-compatible learning.* San Diego, California: The Brain Store.

Jensen, Eric. 1998. *Teaching with the brain in mind.* Alexandria, Virginia: Association for Supervision and Curriculum Development.

Lipton, Laura and Bruce M. Wellman. 1998. *Pathways to understanding: Patterns and practices in the learning-focused classroom.* Guilford, Vermont: Pathways Publishing.

Maxwell Rhoda J. 1996. *Writing across the curriculum in middle and high schools.* Boston: Allyn & Bacon.

Parry, Terence and Gayle Gregory. 1998. *Designing brain compatible learning.* Arlington Heights, Illinois: Skylight Training and Publishing, Inc.

Sousa, David A. 2001. *How the brain learns: A classroom teacher's guide.* Thousand Oaks, California: Corwin Press, Inc.

Wolfe, Patricia. 2001. *Brain matters: Translating research into classroom practice.* Alexandria, Virginia: Association for Supervision and Curriculum Development.

❊ ❊ ❊

# Making Higher Education "Brain-Compatible"

*Jeanette Nunnelley*
*Education*

I have been heavily involved in scholarly endeavors for "brain-compatible classrooms" for the elementary and secondary school for a number of years. Because of tremendous strides in medicine, such as brain imaging techniques, knowledge about the physiological apparatus for learning (the student's brain) has absolutely exploded. We know that learning takes place within the context of other biological systems and is extremely complex. For example, research on the brain has discovered that emotions have a tremendous impact on the production of various neurotransmitters that can either inhibit or enhance the processes associated with learning and memory. To ignore these findings is similar to physicians ignoring the latest advances in medicine and continuing to practice as they were taught 30 years ago.

Neuroscientists, such as Marian Diamond and Janet Hopson (1999), have provided the foundations for what is termed an "enriched environment" that can be applied to all classrooms—from preschool to college. Educators such as Eric Jensen (1998, 2000) Geoffrey and Renate Caine (1991, 1997, 1998), David Sousa (1995, 2001) and Robert Sylwester (1995, 2000) have provided further guidance on translating findings from allied disciplines into educational strategies. Many of these practices affirm and validate what all good teachers at all levels of education have been doing for years; some dictate changes in the pedagogy associated with higher education.

## Recognizing the Impact of Emotions on Learning and the Reality of "Downshifting"

"Complex learning is enhanced by challenge and inhibited by threat associated with a sense of helplessness or fatigue" (Caine, Caine, and Crowell 1999, 195). When there is low challenge or high threat, students are likely to "downshift" to more primitive and instinctive responses (Caine and Caine 1998). A "challenge" is one in which a student is personally engaged and therefore probably intrinsically motivated to accomplish. When students downshift, they revert to early programmed responses of "fight" or "flight" and lose access to higher order thinking skills. The lecture-test, lecture-test, lecture-test routine that is so entrenched in colleges and universities is often boring and only challenges students to stay awake. Exclusively utilizing tests to assess learning is extremely threatening for many students. The pedagogy of lecturing and then testing almost guarantees downshifting.

## Enhancing the Emotional Environment and Avoiding Downshifting

Tileson (2000) lists very specific factors that help create an enriched and supportive environment, thus avoiding downshifting. **Creating a sense of belonging** and a caring community of learners should be modeled as well as expected by all college instructors. Simple traits such as kindness, compassion , acceptance of differences and caring for others (even in a one-hour class) boosts the good neurotransmittors that inhibit downshifting and even assist in moving information into long-term memory.

**A high level of support for achievement** can be enhanced through assignments that recognize strengths in all intelligences: verbal-linguistic, artistic, physical, musical and dramatic. There should be choices in every curriculum based on learning styles, and multiple intelligences.

**A sense of empowerment** is achieved in classrooms where students have choices in assignments that authentically assess their knowledge and skills regardless of the discipline. Teaching strategies that actively involve students such as role playing, debates, case studies, and presentations not only offer challenge but a way for students to authentically demonstrate their learning. Exams hold students accountable, but there are many other beneficial methods of assessment. Finally, lively discussions, rather than a lecture, provide social interactions about a topic, encourage retention, and promote intrinsic motivation.

Brain-based instruction at any educational level revitalizes experienced teachers and enlightens new ones; it affirms best practices and energizes classrooms. The inspired and knowledgeable instructor creates an appropriate emotional environment in which all the physiological forces come together to foster learning.

## References:

Caine, Renate Nummela and Geoffrey Caine. 1991. *Making connections: Teaching and the human brain.* Alexandria, Virginia: Association for Supervision and Curriculum Development.

Caine, Renate Nummela and Geoffrey Caine. 1997. *Education on the edge of possibility.* Alexandria, Maryland: Association for Supervision and Curriculum Development.

Caine, Renate Nummela and Geoffrey Caine. 1998. How to think about the brain. *School Administrator* 55, no. 1:12-16.

Caine, Renate Nummela, Geoffrey Caine and Sam Crowell. (1999). *Mindshifts: A braincompatible process for professional development and the renewal of education,* 2d ed. Tuscon, Arizona: Zephyr Press.

Diamond, Marian Cleeves and Janet L. Hopson. 1999. *Magic trees of the mind: How to nurture your child's intelligence, creativity, and healthy emotions from birth through adolescence.* New York: Plume.

Jensen, E. 2000. *Brain-based learning*, rev. ed. San Diego, California: The Brain Store.

Sousa, David A. 1995. *How the brain learns: A classroom teacher's guide.* Reston, Virginia: National Association of Secondary School Principals.

Sousa, David A. 2001. *How the brain learns: A Classroom teacher's guide,.* 2d ed. Thousand Oaks, California: Corwin Press.

Sylwester, Robert. 2000. Unconscious emotions, conscious feelings. *Educational Leadership* 58, no. 3: 20-24.

Tileston, Donna Walker. 2000. *10 best teaching practices: how brain research, learning styles, and standards define teaching competencies.* Thousand Oaks, California: Corwin Press.

❊ ❊ ❊

## Good Practice and Good Intentions

*S. Holly Stocking*
*Journalism*
*Indiana University Bloomington*

Often when things go wrong, people will say, "Well, at least I meant well." To many of us, it sounds like an excuse. The proof, we counter, is in the pudding, or – in the case of classroom teaching – in the learning. Intention isn't good enough; it's what we students manage to learn that matters. This is the thrust of the recent emphasis on learning over teaching.

It's a good emphasis, a needed emphasis as an antidote to the traditional focus on the teacher. But the focus on intended outcomes can obscure the fact that much of what goes on in students' minds lies outside of our control. The truth is, learning works in non-obvious ways sometimes. There are times when what we

> **Good intentions don't need to be just excuses.**

teach inadvertently, without forethought, is what students benefit from the most. There are times when outright resistance to what we have to teach may be exactly what we – or particular students -- need to experience. The truth is, too, that we are human and can't always see what students need.

If things don't turn out the way we expect, or hope, it can be downright dispiriting. Until we remember our intentions. Good intentions don't need to be just excuses. Sometimes, they are all we have, and they are just the salve that assists us to pick up and try again.

✻ ✻ ✻

# Chapter 5:

# Getting Support

*Courses evolve and improve over time*
*based on our knowledge, experiences, and the support*
*that we seek to improve as teachers.*

Kathryn Ernstberger

## Making Use of Available Support Resources

*Kathryn Ernstberger*
*Business & Economics*
*Indiana University Southeast*

Teaching opportunities for graduate students during a doctoral program are often limited to lower-level courses that follow a departmental syllabus and use a common text book that has already been selected. Thus, the teaching responsibilities that we face during our first years in a tenure-track position may seem very consuming and sometimes overwhelming.

During my first year on the faculty, I taught several courses at both the undergraduate and MBA levels. Not only were all of the courses new preparations for me, some were new to our curriculum. I had never selected my own text book, much less developed my own course. Teaching during that first year demanded most of my time and energy. I suspect the burden would have been considerably lessened had I been aware of the tremendous amount of teaching support that is available. I hope that by writing this, I can alert other new faculty to some of the resources available to us.

The first place to seek input is from your **colleagues** at your new school. Faculty who have already taught the same course are ready to share syllabi, text book recommendations, and sample assignments as well as valuable guidance on how to make the course a successful one. Colleagues in the discipline who teach related courses (especially courses that follow yours) can let you know what their expectations are for the course content. Faculty who serve on a curriculum committee can help you understand the role of your course in the overall curriculum. Your faculty colleagues can also help you understand what kind of student will be in your class. Your new students may be considerably different from those whom you taught in the past and you must be ready to adapt to your new environment.

Many universities now have **teaching resource centers** that serve to support our teaching activities and assist in faculty development in teaching . These centers offer workshops, special teaching libraries, one-on-one consultation, and many other types of support. Their web pages can direct us to important websites such as those for the Professional and Organizational Development Network in Higher Education <http://www.podnetwork.org/> , the National Teaching and Learning Forum <http://www.ntlf.com/>, the ERIC Clearinghouse on Higher Education <http://www.eriche.org/>, and the Society for Teaching and Learning in Higher Education <http://www.tss.uoguelph.ca/stlhe/>. The teaching resource center is a fairly new concept on my campus, and I find that the support services are invaluable and incredibly convenient.

**Professional organizations** also offer a variety of teaching support. I subscribe to a teaching journal that is published by one of my professional organizations. I participate in their annual conferences where I attend the curriculum workshops, peruse and compare the many textbooks that are displayed in the exhibit hall, and make a point of meeting faculty from other universities who teach courses that are similar to mine. I always come away from these meetings with several ideas for my

> **The [teaching] burden would have been considerably lessened had I been aware of the tremendous amount of teaching support that is available.**

classes. **Accrediting agencies** are another source of input on curricular issues. They frequently offer conferences, seminars, and publications that may be helpful.

As a new faculty member, I was most surprised by the support offered by **textbook** publishers. The sales representatives had never bothered to call on me when I was a doctoral student, and I was shocked to find how willing they were to send me complimentary texts to review. In addition, I had no idea that there were so many ancillaries that accompany books: instructor's manuals, solution manuals, test banks, case books, electronic presentation material… While I don't recommend using just the material that a publisher provides, it does help generate ideas and ease the burden of new preparations. In time, you can make the course more your own. Publishers also now provide web sites that contain sample syllabi, on-line testing, grading software, and many other course management materials.

No course will ever be perfect or completely developed. They evolve and improve over time based on our knowledge, experiences, and the support that we seek to improve as teachers. Nonetheless, the process of developing courses is easier if we make use of the resources available to us.

❊ ❊ ❊

## Paired Teaching

*Scott Sernau*
*Sociology*
*Indiana University South Bend*

A very effective way to share and develop teaching techniques is through paired teaching between new and more senior faculty. This pairing expands on the idea of mentoring through classroom visits and recognizes that the learning can go in both directions. New faculty can learn a great deal from master teachers about pacing and presentation, classroom organization and presence, effective use of class time, and how to handle new situations. At the same time, senior faculty can often learn a great deal from new faculty who may arrive fresh from graduate school or other teaching assignments with new ideas about pedagogy, content, and new awareness of emerging teaching techniques.

Pairing can take the form of team teaching in which a new faculty person and a senior faculty member work together on a single course, combining their ideas for readings, topics and approaches. This is probably the most complete and effective form of pairing, since the two faculty must work closely together as teaching colleagues and bring a teaching dialogue into the classroom to be effective. It is also the most time intensive, and campuses differ in their willingness to support team teaching. The course may need to be offered twice, perhaps the first time with the senior faculty member as the "lead" teacher, that is the one getting credit for the course and then a second time with the new faculty person as the "lead." Faculty in the history department on our campus have

> **A very effective way to share and develop teaching techniques is through paired teaching.**

recently used this approach to share ideas and work together in developing a course on African American history.

A second way to work a pairing is with faculty who will be teaching the same courses in different semesters. In the Sociology department, two of our faculty share responsibility for teaching a methods course and a statistics course, with one teaching each course each semester. When the second faculty person arrived, she worked closely with the current person teaching these courses. In one semester he would consult on her methods course and she on his statistics course, and in the next semester the roles were reversed. The senior faculty contributed important ideas in using Web technology and computer exercises, while the junior faculty person contributed important ideas in group learning, and both had ideas about books and resources as well working with "math phobic" students.

The most accessible way to do pairing may be by arranging visits to similar courses. One arrangement this year will have a new person, an anthropologist with an interest in gender, visiting a course on gender roles taught by a sociologist. The more senior person has written articles and compiled resources on teaching about gender, sexuality, and gender roles. The new person can gain a great deal by observing how this research and experience are put into practice in the classroom by a master teacher. At the same time, she is teaching a course on global and cross-cultural perspectives on gender and sexuality. The more senior person is interested in internationalizing her course work and can draw insights from visiting the new person's course. In the spring this new person, who has done field work in Africa, will teach a course on the cultures of Africa. A more senior faculty person (in this case myself) will visit this course, while she will visit my course on international inequalities and global issues. I am eager to expand my coverage of Africa, the continent least known to my students, and to learn from an "Africanist." At the same time, I have worked out ways of engaging students in international issues and thinking globally that I can share with the new person.

Each of these pairing approaches breaks down the isolation that a new person, or a long-timer for that matter, may experience. It allows for mentoring, but also makes this more of a two-way process. It's a reminder to each that we can always learn from one another. The easiest way to establish a program like this is if the department makes a paired teaching experience a regular part of new faculty development. A new person can, however, also suggest this to a department chair or a receptive senior faculty member. With the latter two formats described here, no special arrangements are needed, and the commitment can range from a full semester down to a couple of class visits. Those who have tried this almost always agree that it was time well spent in faculty development.

❈ ❈ ❈

## Is There a Mentor in the House?

*Lori Montalbano-Phelps*
*Communication*
*Indiana University Northwest*

As a new teacher (first semester), I felt I had to do everything right, and if mistakes were made, I had to keep that to myself. At times

> Mentoring allows for the sharing of ideas, emotions... reflections [and resources] from those who can directly relate to your experience.

this resulted in sleepless nights and uncertainty during the next class meeting. I went along, journaling and trying to problem-solve by myself, but I was missing out on experiencing a wonderful resource right in my back-yard: my colleagues who were filled with experience and anecdotes for every occasion. As I began to openly reflect on my concerns and aspirations for my classes, I found many seasoned teachers willing to talk and offer advice. I learned that it's okay to make mistakes, just learn from them. I learned that perfection in the classroom is something to reach for, but not to expect. I learned that self-criticism can be the worst. I learned that students appreciate an instructor who is being "real,"and that you don't have to be a superhero–just be yourself.

Mentoring allows for the sharing of ideas, emotions and reflections from those who can directly relate to your experience. It allows for the sharing of resources. I now work closely with other faculty to offer support, to share ideas that I have found successful in my classes, and to share class materials such as exams, syllabi, and activities. Perhaps most importantly, I will openly share with other faculty those strategies that didn't work as effectively as I'd hoped. Above all, when I work with other faculty, I try to demonstrate my love for teaching and learning. I remember some of the most influential teachers I had over the years. They inspired me because of their dedication to students and their love of learning. They were enthusiastic, concerned for students, and cared whether I understood the material. When I mentor others about teaching, I find myself referencing these qualities that have made such a difference in my teaching approaches. I urge you to seek out those who are willing to share ideas and serve as mentors to you. A collaborative faculty can build strong relationships that nurture teaching effectiveness and support for students *and* colleagues.

**References:**
Austin, Ann E. & Baldwin, Roger G. 1991. *Faculty collaboration: Enhancing the quality of scholarship and teaching.* Washington D.C.: George Washington University Press.

Enerson, Diane M. 2001. Mentoring as metaphor: An opportunity for innovation and renewal. *New Directions for Teaching and Learning* 85: 7-15.

Harnish, Dorothy and Lynn A.1994. Mentoring strategies for faculty development. *Studies in Higher Education* 19, no.2: 191-201.

Pierce, Gloria. 1998. Developing new university faculty through mentoring. *Journal of Humanistic Education and Development* 37, no.1: 27-40.

Sorcinelli, Mary D. 1994. Effective approaches to new faculty development. *Journal of Counseling and Development* 72, no. 5: 474-480.

St. Clair, Karen L. 1994. Faculty-to-faculty mentoring in the community college: An instructional component of faculty. *Community College Review* 22, no.3: 23-36.

❈ ❈ ❈

## Book an Appointment @ Your Library
*Michele C. Russo*
*Franklin D. Schurz Library*
*Indiana University South Bend*

You're new on campus and there is so much to learn (finding where your classrooms are and where to get a parking permit will be high on your list) and so much to do (including filling out W-4 forms, selecting an insurance plan, and getting your syllabi ready before the first day of classes). You'll be bombarded with faculty and student handbooks, departmental policies, and days of orientation that will leave you bleary-eyed. In the midst of all of this, you may overlook getting to know some people who can help you get the year started off right with your teaching and research. I am, of course, talking about your friendly, helpful librarians.

If you've just completed your PhD program, you may well be thinking that you know about libraries and all the resources you use. Why should you take time out of an already hectic schedule to make an appointment with a librarian when you already know about libraries? The answer is quite simple: no two libraries are exactly alike in the resources or services that they offer or the policies that they have. More importantly, though, your librarians can be of significant help to you in your teaching and research. It's well worth your time to get acquainted.

As director of a library, I make a point of inviting each new faculty member to meet individually with me and a couple of other librarians. I know that new faculty are all very busy at the beginning of the semester, but I encourage them to make this appointment within the first two to three weeks of classes. After that, they'll *really* be busy. If you don't get an invitation from your librarian, I'd suggest that you invite yourself. If you're at a large, research institution, you'll probably want to meet with your subject bibliographer. If you're at a smaller or medium sized institution, just begin at the top with the director and that person will be sure to introduce you to the other librarians and staff you need to know.

At the meetings that I hold, we always begin by asking the new faculty members about their area of research and what courses they will be teaching. Of course, we want to know how they use the library for their own research and in their classes. With those answers in mind, we can tell them about the resources and services we offer that they should know about. If you're initiating the meeting, here are some questions you may want to ask, beginning with the obvious circulation policies and moving to services and specific resources:

Do you need a separate library card or will your faculty ID work?

How long can you check out materials?

Do periodicals circulate?

Can your research assistant check out materials for you?

You know that reference librarians are available to help you and your students at the reference desk, but will they also come to your office?

Do they take questions over email?

Will they work with you to design "research assignments" for your classes?
Consulting with librarians on assignments helps ensure that you don't ask students to use resources that the Library doesn't have.

> **Librarians want to do
> all that they can to help
> you and your students succeed.**

What kind of research instruction for your classes do they offer? (Remember, just because you know how to do research doesn't mean that your students do. They can probably use some help getting started in the process. Also, remember that interfaces change, new sources become available, and it's unlikely you'll be able to keep up without help from the librarians. You don't want to give wrong or outdated information to your students about the library.) If you teach at an off-campus site, will the librarians come to there to give instruction?

83

What kind of services do they offer for off-site students?

Find out about Interlibrary Loan/ Document Delivery service. No library has everything that you need, so the ILL folks can quickly become your best friends. Does the library have arrangements with other academic libraries in the area that would allow you to borrow directly from them?

What are the reserves policies? Does the library offer electronic reserves?

Is there someone in the Library who can help with copyright questions (both for use of materials in classroom and for your publications)?

Last, but certainly not least, what resources does the Library have that you consider essential?

If you're at a research institution, the library will likely have the major resources for your area of research (but be aware, as noted above, that electronic resources may not be available in the same interface that you're used to). Smaller libraries may not have the specialized sources you need. Talk with the librarians about whether they'd be able to purchase them for you. Or are there alternative sources that you may not be aware of? What are the policies and procedures for suggesting additions to the collection? Can you add new serials and non-print items?

At many institutions, librarians have faculty status and have been through the tenure process. Even if they haven't, they've been sure to help other faculty on their way. What tips can they give you that you may not hear from your department?

While the answers to all of these questions may vary from place to place, there is one thing that you can count on: librarians want to do all that they can to help you and your students succeed. Make a point of getting to know them. It will definitely be worth your time.

I'm certain that there is no need to convince you of the importance of using libraries for your own research. However, I would like to emphasize the importance of collaboration between teaching faculty and librarians in order to help improve the academic performance of their students. Below is a listing of some of the research on this topic.

**References:**

Breivik, Patricia Senn. 1998. *Student learning in the information age*. Phoenix, Arizona: American Council on Education/Oryx Press.

Evans, Ruby. 2001. Faculty and reference librarians: A virtual dynamic duo. An internal educational partnership for learning. *T.H.E. Journal* 28, no. 6 (Jan): 46, 48-51.

Gilson, Caroline and Stephanie Michel. 2002. Fishing for success: faculty/librarian collaboration nets effective library assignments. In *Making the grade: Academic libraries and student success*, ed. Maurie Caitlin Kelly and Andrea Kross. Chicago: Association of College and Research Libraries.

Huerta, Deborah and Victoria E. McMillan. 2000. Collaborative instruction by writing and library faculty: A two-tiered approach to the teaching of scientific writing. *Issues in Science & Technology Librarianship* 28 (Fall).

Raspa, Dick and Dane Ward, eds. 2000. *The collaborative imperative: Librarians and faculty working together in the information universe*. Chicago: Association of College and Research Libraries.

❋ ❋ ❋

## Preparing to Teach

*Erv Boschman*
*Chemistry*
*Indian Universit- Purdue University Indianapolis*

**I was least prepared for what I was to do most: TEACH**

Fresh out of graduate school, my chairman introduced me to the class of 120 eager souls – then promptly left. That day I delivered my semi-memorized lecture, wishing I could trade places with the janitor down the hall. He was whistling a happy tune and looked like he enjoyed his job. Furthermore, I was certain that his knees were steady and his mouth was not puckered and dry.

That first semester, I frequently walked in a nearby park, wrestling with my calling. Now, I'm glad I didn't give up on teaching. The pain was severe at times, but the rewards have been immeasurably high.

What can I share that might be of some help? After reflection, I have prepared some survival tips gathered from my teaching experience:

**Ask someone to be your mentor**. You are now a teacher, but the mentor will give you a chance to be a listener and student again.

**Make use of workshops.** I suggest you participate in at least four or five. Workshops deal with topics such as diversity, promotion and tenure, grant writing, and copyright laws.

**If you want to teach math to Mary, get to know Mary**. Student surveys repeatedly show that the top attributes of respected teachers are care, enthusiasm, and knowledge – in that order.

Spend time with your family. Let me repeat: Spend time with your family.

I was least prepared for what I was to do most: TEACH.

❋ ❋ ❋

# Chapter 6:

# Lessons From the Disciplines

*"Teachers will be most effective
if they maintain their own personal identity and integrity
while being guided by the tenets of pedagogy."*
**Kindsvatter, Willen, and Ishler (1996)**

## Improving Quality of Study Time

*Donna Dahlgren*
*Psychology*
*Indiana University Southeast*

Substantial research has uncovered little relationship between absolute amount of time studying for exams and subsequent exam scores (see, for example, Rau and Durant 2000). I pursued this relationship in an Introductory Psychology course by periodically asking students to reflect on how much time they spent studying and what their expectations were regarding exam grades. As with previous research, I discovered only a moderate relationship between absolute number of hours studied and exam score. In addition, students who scored below their own expectations on exams were not necessarily inclined to increase their study time for subsequent exams.

---

**Increased study time, by itself, may not lead to better exam scores.**

---

A sizable research literature has revealed that the type, or (Craik and Lockhart 1972). The implications of this well documented fact are enormous for college students. Simply asking our students to study more is an insufficient means of improving their academic performance. Instead, some measure of the quality of study strategies used is necessary. A better measure of study strategies would have given me better information about the quality of my students' studying. In the future, I intend to implement a study skills checklist that students can complete indicating how they studied for the exam. Because students may be unaware that increased study time, by itself, may not lead to better exam scores, faculty would be well advised to emphasize the importance of developing more effective study strategies. For my own students, I recommend the following strategies:

> Applying material to personal experience
> Teaching material to others
> Interrupt reading frequently with reflective questions
> Take notes while reading, using their own words and paraphrasing material

**References:**

Craik, Fergus I. and Robert S. Lockhart. 1972. Levels of processing: A framework for memory research. *Journal of Verbal Learning and Verbal Behavior* 11: 671-684.

Rau, William and Ann Durand. 2000. The academic ethic and college grades: Does hard work help students to "make the grade"? *Sociology of Education* 73: 19-38.

※ ※ ※

## Something Old, Something New: A Twist on the Traditional Term Paper

*Gretchen L. Anderson*
*Chemistry*
*Indiana University South Bend*

Although there are a wide variety of ways to increase students' learning, motivation, and interest, new faculty who are unfamiliar with these techniques may prefer to make incremental adjustments in their teaching rather than embracing radical changes. New faculty are usually most comfortable teaching in the style in which they themselves have been taught, which usually means new faculty continue with the basic lecture format. However, it is well established that true learning comes not from simply assimilating myriad facts from a lecture and textbook, but from applying knowledge, critically evaluating information from various sources and using this knowledge to generate informed decisions or opinions (Bruner).

Traditionally, many lecture courses have addressed this issue by including a term paper requirement. In the process of writing the term paper, students are engaged in active learning, particularly if the assignment includes formation of an opinion on a controversial issue. To prepare the term paper, students gather information, sift through conflicting data, analyze and critically evaluate source material, and eventually come to an opinion or thesis that forms the crux of the term paper. If the term paper topic is appropriately chosen, students must critically evaluate the material they have researched according to the primary course content, and develop an informed opinion about the topic. Once this learning process is accomplished, students organize the information and compose sentences and paragraphs to communicate their knowledge and ideas. This writing component of the paper is very useful for increasing writing skills and helping students communicate their ideas. The term paper thus engages learners for all intents and purposes in a basic form of an inquiry activity that requires analysis, synthesis, and evaluation of new ideas. By assigning term papers, new faculty can maintain the comfort of traditional teaching methods while they gradually experiment with other processes of active learning.

Although term papers provide a means for students to engage in one form of active learning, there are several disadvantages. Generally, the student is able to improve his or her skills in proportion to the amount of feedback from the instructor (Day 1989) . Students' knowledge may be masked by their

> **New faculty may prefer to make incremental adjustments in their teaching.**

poor writing ability, particularly in lower level undergraduate classes. Furthermore, it takes a great deal of time on the instructor's part to adequately grade and annotate term papers. New faculty can be overwhelmed by the amount of time required for grading term papers.

**The term paper outline**

The term paper outline is a compromise that retains many of the positive attributes of inquiry learning but requires much less time to evaluate. For this exercise, students turn in a detailed outline of the term paper, but do not complete the writing of the paper. To construct the outline, students must still find information, assimilate the facts, evaluate the quality of the sources, organize concepts and form opinions or a thesis. By writing an outline, students perform the first set of activities involved in effective communication and gain feedback on this important building block of constructing a term paper or other written work.

The advantages of this approach are numerous for both faculty and students. Faculty will find that grading outlines is a time-effective way to assess student learning. I have found that I can grad outlines in one fourth to one third the time required to grade comparable term papers. Assigning several outlines per semester then becomes more practical and gives students a chance to improve their skills as well as use this form of active inquiry learning on several topics for the course. Even in moderately large classes (60-70 students), I can adequately comment on each outline to ensure students get the feedback they need for continuing improvement. Comments can be directed towards the students' understanding of the material content, their classification of facts and their critical evaluation without nearly as much comment for sentence structure, grammar and syntax. The use of phrases is easier for the reader to understand so that time is not spent trying to analyze poorly structured sentences.

Because outlines consist of organized phrases rather than complete sentences, there are several ancillary benefits. I find that incidences of plagiarism are drastically reduced. The outline forces students to write their own synopses of information gathered and to arrange the phrases according to the outline topics. This helps them understand the material they are reading, restate the concepts in their own wording and evaluate how this material relates to other facts or concepts. Rather than copying or slightly modifying sentences from the original source, students must reformat the material to fit the outline. In addition, phrases are easier to check for factual accuracy since they cannot be lost in a convoluted sentence structure. Use of phrases in the outline format also has the effect of improving the rhetoric and tone of the outline. I see far less bellicosity and exaggeration in the outlines than in term papers.

Perhaps most importantly, for those students who are poor writers because they do not outline, this activity provides a chance for them to practice organizing complex material and making accurate and appropriate connections. Since the outline is the end product, students will not engage in the common practice of free association in narrative form. Instead they are more likely to focus on exactly the constructivist skills the term paper ideally addresses.

**Making it work**

Flexibility is the key to making it work. Outlines can be very useful for organizing ideas, even if they are not in a formal format. For example, I do not require Roman numerals or other numbering systems, as long as the indented ideas are related to the heading above it. I allow a single subheading under a heading, especially if it is an example to illustrate the point.

Many students are unfamiliar or uncomfortable with making outlines, and I encountered some initial dubiousness. I provide not only a rubric I will be using for grading the outlines, but also a model outline on a topic ancillary to our course material, and a sample of a graded outline, complete with comments and a grade. To ensure high quality in the outlines, I also emphasize the importance of rhetoric and appearance. Spelling, grammar, and mature tone are easy for students to address if they know it is important to the instructor. For the types of topics I assign, references are important, and proper listing of references or a bibliography is a part of the grading rubric.

One of the goals for assigning outlines is for students to gain experience with this organizational approach to other writing assignments in outer courses. I stress the importance of organization by weighting it quite heavily in the grading of the outline.

> **New faculty can be overwhelmed by the amount of time required for grading term papers.**

Introducing the concept of the outline takes about 10 minutes of class time when combined with a rubric and a graded model outline. The first outlines students hand in are generally good; once they get feedback from their first outline, subsequent outlines are of very high quality.

**Use of outlines in chemistry courses**

I have used outlines very effectively in entry level survey chemistry courses. The focus of these courses is to relate chemistry concepts to everyday situations. Weekly topics usually involve controversial societal issues involving chemistry. Students find information (in practice, almost exclusively from the internet), and put it together with chemical concepts learned in class lectures. Students then shape an informed opinion, backed up with facts, and in outline form they present their knowledge, acknowledge the valid arguments on both sides of an issue, indicate how they weighed conflicting data, and provide a list of references.

When I assigned only short persuasive papers, it was evident that students at this level often lacked the tools to write cogent paragraphs. To address this, the following year I asked students to provide an outline and then a short paper on the same topic as the outline. Although I saw this as a great way to force organization of the paper, most of the students viewed these as two separate assignments. The paper rarely had any recognizable relationship to the outline. Many students said they wrote the paper first, and then wrote the outline. I concluded that these students were not viewing an outline as the starting point for writing a paper. The following year I therefore assigned only the outline, and reaped the benefits of decreased grading time. Typically, I assign four outlines on controversial issues (*e.g.* whether the dangers of genetically modified foods outweigh their benefits, or whether olestra-containing products should be available to the public).

I have been very pleased with the outline format. For a chemistry class, it is a powerful way to assess students' understanding of underlying science, and their ability to apply scientific principles to controversial social issues. For students, it provides a valuable opportunity to gather and critically evaluate information, and express an informed opinion. With more experience students should be much more comfortable with using outlines as a basis for writing formal essays or term papers. For new faculty, the outline provides a means of addressing some of the fundamental skills in achieving high levels of cognition without losing the comfort and familiarity of traditional teaching methods. Most importantly, this is accomplished without an inordinate amount of time expended in grading. This method of merging older formats of college teaching (*i.e.* content-rich lectures) with newer approaches to active learning and critical thinking may be a suitable way for new faculty to incorporate more constructivist teaching and learning in their courses.

**References:**

Bruner, Jerome S. 1966. *Toward a theory of instruction.* Cambridge, Massachusetts: Harvard University Press.

Day, Susan. 1989. Producing better writers in sociology classes: A test of the writing-across-the curriculum approach. *Teaching Sociology* 17: 458-64.

❊ ❊ ❊

## This Isn't an Art Class, But That Doesn't Preclude Creativity

*Betsy Lucal*
*Sociology*
*Indiana University South Bend*

After participating in a workshop my colleague Marsha Heck (IUSB, School of Education) gave on infusing art into the curriculum, I decided to try my hand at getting students' artistic and creative juices flowing. In Sociology of Oppression and Privilege and Sociology of Women, I gave students the opportunity to create a representation of some part of the course content that did not rely on words. Students created collages, dioramas and other three-dimensional representations. To help ensure

> **Creative projects give students the chance to...explore the course content in a different way.**

that I was interpreting their creative products as they had intended, they also turned in a one-page description of the meaning of their project. These creative projects give students the chance to move away from the traditional academic paper and to explore the course content in a different way.

❋ ❋ ❋

## The Nature of "Reality": How Theories Color Our View of the World Around Us

*Jerry Powers*
*Social Work*
*Indiana University-Purdue University Indianapolis*

Every once in a while in the course of our formal education, we are fortunate enough to experience what is sometimes referred to as a

"transforming learning moment". I recall one such experience when I was a freshman in high school. I was taking a beginning biology course from an enormously talented teacher by the name of Sister William Elizabeth.

I recall quite vividly the "experiment of the day" in which the class was asked to examine closely a specimen under a microscope (as I recall it, that specimen was a cross-section of a leaf pressed between two pieces of glass). The immediate object of the assignment was to examine the specimen and replicate it as closely as possible in a full color rendering on a piece of paper. Once having completed that task, each student was required to display his/her drawing for the benefit of the class as a whole.

When the initial picture was completed, each student was given an optical lens of a different color to insert in the microscope. Without modifying the position or angle of the specimen in any way, the exercise was then repeated with the same set of instructions – "Draw and color the specimen exactly as you see it." After replicating the assignment as observed through a rose colored lens, we were required to repeat the task several additional times with the sole variation of viewing the specimen through a variety of different colored lenses.

When the experiment was completed, each student had on display a set of five different renderings of the same specimen as seen through the microscope in relation to five different colored lenses. As someone who prided myself on the compulsive nature of my ability to draw, naively I remember feeling a special sense of personal satisfaction that I had done especially well on the assignment because I felt my drawings provided accurate representations of each aspect of the assignment. Needless to say, I was at once both surprised and chagrined to learn that the purpose of the assignment had nothing to do with how well we could draw!

When all of the students had completed the task of drawing and coloring each version of the specimen as seen through the various colored lenses, Sister "Willy" (as we fondly caller her) posed one of those confounding questions that forever transformed the way I have viewed the world – *"Which of the drawings represents reality?"*

> **Each view provided us with a unique yet meaningful view of...reality.**

As one might imagine, the discussion that followed was both lively and heated with each student giving her/his best argument on behalf of one or other of the competing drawings. Some students argued that the specimen as viewed through the so-called "clear lens" provided the most accurate representation of reality since it was "uncontaminated by the color imposed by the other lenses. Others argued that the relative merits of one or other of the "colored" views since they seemed to add something that could not be seen through the "clear" lens.

What became apparent to everyone, however, was the fact that each of the experiments provided an alternative way of viewing the same specimen. Each lens enabled the "researcher" to see a different "reality". What was clearly visible with one lens seemed to disappear when viewed through the prism of one of the other lenses. Certain features of the specimen that were totally absent when viewed through a green lens seemed to come into sharp relief when viewed through an amber colored lens. Similarly, the green lens heightened awareness of features that could not be seen through the amber lens. And so it was with all of the lenses – "reality" seemed to change with each iteration of the experiment. Was it that one view was more accurate than the others, or could it be that each view provided us with a unique yet meaningful view of the reality we had been attending to?

When all was said and done, we discovered that theories are not unlike the multi-colored lenses through which we had viewed this microscopic cross-section of a leaf. In a sense they provide different color prisms through which we view our world, each bringing into sharp relief certain features at the expense of others. Consequently, theories should never be judged in terms of being *true* or *false*. They are simply more or less useful depending upon the context in which they are applied. While it is certainly possible to be unaware of the theories (and by extension our personal biases) that inform our world view, it is impossible not to be influenced, at least implicitly, by the theories that color the way we see our world. They inevitably color and define our view of the people and things around us. Sister William Elizabeth knew that fact better than most folks and she shared that transforming insight with her students in a very special way.

※ ※ ※

# Writing Dialogues to Enhance Student Learning
# in Introductory Ethics Classes

*Louise Collins*
*Philosophy*
*Indiana University South Bend*

Introductory students often find discussing controversial moral issues challenging, both intellectually and emotionally. When asked why someone might disagree with one of their deeply-held moral beliefs, e.g., that abortion is wrong, students often produce an explanation of someone's holding the belief, e.g., "Well, I guess if they were brought up atheist, they would think abortion is no big deal"and find it hard to imagine that there might be reasons at work also.

If they can imagine a reason at all, it's likely to be a weak one, "If you think it's OK to murder the weak and defenseless, then I guess you'd have no problem with abortion." Clearly, this is a weak reason, and it is certainly not a reason given by supporters of abortion rights in defense of their position. Encouraging students to explore how others might have (at least prima facie) good reasons for their different moral beliefs is important. It helps foster an attitude of tolerance towards others' beliefs in the classroom; and it helps students avoid the Straw Man fallacy in defending their own beliefs.

A technique I use is to divide students into groups, with the task of writing a dialogue on a controversial moral topic. Each dialogue must have at least three characters and run a specified minimum number of lines. The group is to assign each character a position on the topic – e.g., "Abortion is always wrong"; "Abortion can sometimes be morally acceptable"; "Abortion is always morally permissible"-- and write a script for each character. Students can invent a profile for their characters, e.g., a name, an occupation, an open-minded or dogmatic style of conversing.

The groups then perform the dialogue for the class, and the "actors" respond to audience questions about their beliefs in character. The assignment gets a group grade for the dialogue as a whole, and then each individual submits (in their personal voice) an account of what they think about the issue, on balance. The dialogue task thus requires students literally to voice the reasoning of someone with whom they disagree.

The "dialogue" task can be varied, e.g., to require each group to work into their characters' mouths four assigned logical fallacies, and see if the rest of the class spots the fallacy as it is committed.

I allow some in-class time for the groups to start working on the project; but I expect that most of it will be done outside class. It's an advantage of this group project that it can be accomplished easily by e-mail or Oncourse, if students can't coordinate to meet physically.

I often assign this group project to follow an individual bibliography/research assignment which requires students to identify and evaluate resources in specific categories (e.g., a web site, an academic journal article, an on-line encyclopedia, etc.). The dialogue and the list of resources would both be focused on the same moral issue.

> **Encouraging students to explore how others might have... good reasons for their different moral beliefs...helps foster an attitude of tolerance.**

✳ ✳ ✳

# Linking Mathematics with Computer & Information Technology

*Morteza Shafii-Mousavi*
*Mathematics*
*Indiana University South Bend*

*Paul Kochanowski*
*Business and Economics*
*Indiana University South Bend*

We linked two subject areas to integrate subjects taught in traditional sections of finite mathematics with skills and concepts acquired in traditional sections of introduction to computers and information technology. Placing these related subjects in parallel, we emphasized the linkages and practical applications between the two components, much like what has been done in IUSB Connections (Shafii-Mousavi and Smith 2002).

An interdisciplinary project-based course Mathematics in Action: Social and Industrial Problems composed of

> M110 Excursion in Mathematics,
> M118 Finite Mathematics, and
> T102 Mathematics for Elementary Teachers 2, was linked to a Computer Technology course composed of
> A106 Introduction to Computing and
> K201 The Computer in Business.

## Mathematics in Action

The primary intent of the course, Mathematics in Action, is to encourage an appreciation of mathematics as students see an immediate use for it in completing actual real-world projects. The course emphasizes learning mathematics through completion of actual industrial group projects. Sources of projects are local organizations such as banks, school corporations, industries, government agencies, and social organizations (Shafii-Mousavi and Kochanowski 2000). Projects are

selected to emphasize finite mathematics tools and are assigned to students who work in teams, with three or four students on each team. To optimize the interaction of students with diverse academic interests, each team consists of students from several disciplines, such as business, nursing, science, education, and public and environmental affairs. Given a particular project, student teams start by formulating research issues, problems, and questions. They then focus on data needs and on acquiring the mathematical, statistical, and computer skills necessary to solve these problems. In the classroom, students learn core mathematical techniques and concepts, which satisfy replaced courses of diverse disciplines, and customized mathematical topics necessary to finish industrial projects. Finally, each team writes a comprehensive report and makes a presentation in class and at its resource organization. The learning activities that take place in working on the projects cut across all disciplines and benefit education majors as much as they do science and business majors.

## Needs for Technology

The use of real data for the projects and the ability to find a solution has highlighted the necessity to use computer technology and modern software. *The Use of Computer Technology in a First-year Finite Mathematics Course* (Shafii-Mousavi and Kochanowski 1999, 344-9) discusses this necessity and our experience of the use of technology. We had not envisioned this need the first time we taught the course. Initially, we had thought that students could use graphing calculators to analyze the data sets for their projects. This was very naive on our part. Many real world projects involve large data sets or large numbers of calculations that simply cannot be done on a hand held calculator. Our delinquency loan rate project for the financial institution, for example, had approximately 140,000 loan accounts for each of twelve months (longer periods were also available). A routing problem using a traveling salesperson algorithm was too large even for the computer, had to be broken into parts, and then reconstructed to obtain solutions. This unexpected need for technology turned out to be a blessing in disguise (though this is not necessarily the way we thought about it that first year). The need to use modern day technology has led to an awareness and appreciation by our students of the power of merging technology and mathematics in solving real world problems. This has become one of the more important learning outcomes from the use of real world projects.

Through this association, students

Gain comprehension of the relevance of the concepts articulated in both areas,

Get better preparation to apply both skill sets in future academic undertakings, Learn finite mathematics in the mathematics component,

Gain basic skills of both information technology and computer software, and

Apply mathematics and computer technology to solve actual projects at actual organizations in the community.

**Projects Illustrating the Linkage between Mathematics and Technology**

This semester, student teams completed actual industrial projects using mathematics and technology. They wrote technical reports and presented solutions for the organizations.

| Industrial Project | Mathematical Skills Used | Technological Skills Used |
|---|---|---|
| *Indirect Loan Risk Analysis* for Teachers Credit Union | Statistical Analysis, Conditional Probabilities, Bayesian Formula, Data Cleansing | Access, Data Base Techniques, EXCEL Spreadsheet, Word Processing |
| *Copying Cost Analysis* for Penn Harris Madison School Corporation | Sampling, Statistics, Linear Cost Functions, Simulation Techniques | EXCEL Spreadsheet, Word Processing |
| *Mail Delivery Routing* for Indiana University South Bend Special Services | Gathering Data, Time & Distance Measurements, Traveling Salesperson Problem, Heuristic Rules | EXCEL Spreadsheet, Lindo/Lingo Software Word Processing |
| *Here Today, Gone Tomorrow* (student retention analysis) for Indiana University South Bend Student Support Services | Survey Techniques, Statistical Analysis, Conditional Probabilities, Bayesian Formula, Data Cleansing | Access, Data Base Techniques, EXCEL Spreadsheet, Word Processing |
| *IUSB Security* for Indiana University South Bend Security Office | Statistical Analysis, Conditional Probabilities, Bayesian Formula, Data Cleansing | Access, Data Base Techniques, EXCEL Spreadsheet, Word Processing |

Student evaluations include traditional exams in both disciplines, industrial projects, and individual projects.

**References:**

Shafii-Mousavi, Morteza and Paul Kochanowski. 2000. How to design and teach a project based first-year finite mathematics course. *The Journal of Undergraduate Mathematics and Its Applications (UMAP)* 21, no. 2: 119-138.

Shafii-Mousavi, Morteza and Paul Kochanowski. 1999. The use of computer technology in a first-year finite mathematics course. In *Mathematics/Science Education Technology*, Charlottesville, Virginia: Association for Advancement of Computing in Education.

Shafii-Mousavi, Morteza and Ken Smith. 2002. *Interdepartmental Collaborations for a Community of Teaching and Learning.* Academic Chairpersons: The Changing Role of Department Chairs, National Issues in Higher Education Series 52: 177-184.

✳ ✳ ✳

## Video, Worksheets, and Classroom Discussion

*Kevin Glowacki*
*Classical Studies*
*Indiana University Bloomington*

When I want to show a videotape in my archaeology class, I carefully preview the film and try to select an appropriate segment of no more than 15-20 minutes in length. If it is necessary to show more than one segment, I make sure to break up the presentation into clearly defined parts, usually by turning on the classroom lights, moving about the room, stressing key points, asking for student feedback, and introducing the next segment. This kind of "change up" helps the students

(and instructor) stay alert (*i.e.,* awake) and distinguishes the classroom activity from the passive mode of watching an archaeology special on cable TV.

For each video, I also prepare a handout with several leading questions and ask the students to write down short answers as they watch the film. The worksheet helps the students to focus on the specific details and concepts that relate to the course material and themes of that day's class, while encouraging them to remain attentive and actively engaged. I find that five or six questions based on the content of the video are more than enough. I also include two other questions at the end: 1) What is the most important thing you learned from the video? 2) What do you still have questions about?

Immediately after the video segment, I raise the lights and give the students a few minutes to complete their worksheets, stressing the importance of their answers to the last two questions. At the beginning of the semester I have the students introduce themselves to those sitting next to them and share their answers before starting a general class discussion. I then know that I can call on any student in the class for a comment on either "What did you learn?" or "What is your question?" By the middle of the semester we usually jump directly to the group "debriefing" and there are rarely any awkward silences.

I also make a point of collecting the worksheets, glancing over their answers and summarizing their questions. (This takes far less time at home or in the office than one might imagine and is an easy way to assess the impact of the video and to notice any mistakes. Moreover, the questions from 100+ students usually fall into only ten or twelve broad categories – which, of course, will be more or less the same the next time you teach the course!). I begin the very next class by handing back the worksheet, reviewing or correcting errors or misconceptions, and answering any questions we did not address the previous day. In this way the video/worksheet combination enhances the learning environment by providing a visually interesting "change up" from the usual format of the class, helps students engage the material and formulate their own opinions and questions, provides the teacher with an effective and efficient method for assessing the impact of the video on student learning, and encourages classroom discussion.

❋ ❋ ❋

## Helping Students to Think About – and Do – "Good Work"

*S. Holly Stocking*
*Journalism*
*Indiana University Bloomington*

> *"People who do good work... are clearly skilled in one or more professional realms. At the same time, rather than merely following money or fame alone, or choosing the path of least resistance when in conflict, they are thoughtful about their responsibilities and the implications of their work."*
>
> Howard Gardner, Mihaly Csikszentmihalyi, and William Damon, *Good Work: When Excellence and Ethics Meet* (Basic Books, 2001)

"Good work," as Gardner and his colleagues (2001) have defined it, can be a sound organizing theme for courses in professional ethics. It can help students to both think about -- and do--good work. In my own course in professional ethics, I help students to think about good work by creating conditions for them to:

**Explore definitions of good work in our professional domain:** Journalism students bring to the class definitions of one dimension of "good work," *technical mastery*, which they have acquired in journalism skills courses; we discuss these definitions. We also examine professional codes and other documents for understandings of media's *social responsibilities and ethics*. As part of these discussions, we begin to raise questions about the complex relationships between excellence, responsibilities and ethics, and commercial "success."

> **The task of comparison demands critical thinking, which students struggle with at first and then come to enjoy.**

**Examine the lives of individual professionals, to see if they are doing "good work":** In a 5-7 page paper, students review the body of work of a media professional of their choosing (someone researched and written about in some depth) and assess the *level of mastery* achieved by that professional. In a second paper, students analyze the professional's work-related *values* and his or her *ethical reasoning* when faced with an ethical problem or dilemma; in this assignment, students are encouraged to use classical ethical theories and other approaches to ethical reasoning learned in the class.

**Analyze the conditions that lead these professionals to do good (or not-so good) work**: In a third paper, students assess the professional's work overall and analyze the many conditions, personal and professional, that have influenced the individual's ability (or inability) to do "good work." These include values of the family of origin, mentors, education and training, organization climate, professional climate, cultural climate, and other influences. In exploring conditions, students begin to think of excellence and ethics not only as matters of individual agency, but also as matters of profoundly interdependent relationships. In this way, students are encouraged to neither lionize nor demonize their professionals, but to discover them in all their interconnected humanity.

**Compare and contrast workers to develop a deeper understanding of what is needed to produce good work in the domain**: In assigned teams of three to five, students compare and contrast professionals and develop a presentation to share their discoveries with the class. The task of comparison demands critical thinking, which students struggle with at first and then come to enjoy. Presentations, which have included improvisational talk shows, simulations, videotaped interviews, game shows, murals, timelines, and maps, exercise students' creative capacities.

I help students to do good work *about* good work by:

**Exploring definitions of good work in our academic domain.** As part of this effort, we discuss technical mastery as defined in our professional curriculum – rigorous standards of coherence, information gathering, analysis and interpretation, organization and composition, and writing and editing. We also read the university's code of ethics on plagiarism and other forms of academic misconduct; for most of the students (all seniors), this is the first time they have read the code.

**Discussing the conditions for good work in an academic setting.** Conditions include (but are not limited to) the *Seven Principles of Good Practice in Undergraduate Education* by Chickering and Gamson (1987) -- time on task, student-faculty contact, and cooperation among students. (Getting enough sleep is also rated as exceedingly important, by everyone!)

**Creating conditions students need to do good work in this class.** Students who aspire to do good work in this class (and not all do) are given the opportunity to rewrite assignments to bring them up to a level of mastery. All are expected to work on an honor system; each time they turn in a paper, students sign a statement that they have not engaged in acts of academic misconduct as defined by the university and that they have passed their own personal "mirror test."

I strive to model good work:

**I myself strive to be technically proficient as a teacher**. That is, I strive to communicate and reinforce high expectations for mastery and integrity; to encourage active learning and participation; to provide prompt feedback; and to offer diverse activities to meet diverse learning styles and engage diverse talents (see Chickering and Gamson, *Seven Principles of Good Practice in Undergraduate Education,* 1987). To learn the material, students engage in simulations, debates, personal reflection, and analysis of excerpts from feature films ("Absence of Malice," and "Broadcast News") that depict journalists in ethical quandaries. Working professionals also discuss their own experiences of "good work" (and not-so-good work) with the class.

**I strive to be fair-minded, with concern for the implications of my methods on student learning.** As one measure of learning, I ask the students to reassess an essay written at the start of the term. This is part of a more extensive evaluation that the students do of their own learning.

Organizing a professional ethics course around the theme of "good work" allows students to consider the complex relationships between technical mastery, responsibilities and ethics, and commercial success. It requires students to not only learn the traditional lessons of a professional ethics class, but also to apply these lessons to an analysis of a particular professional's work. This analysis and the accompanying team project enable students to discover that good work arises out of more than the talents, skills, and values of individuals; it also arises out of the social conditions in which individuals are situated.

As students work to do good work about good work, they put theory into practice. As I work to do good work myself, so do I.

**References:**

Gardner, Howard, Mihaly Csikszentmihalyi, and William Damon. 2001. *Good work: When excellence and ethics meet.* New York: Basic Books.

Chickering, Arthur W. And Zelda F. Gamson. 1987. *Seven principles of good practice in undergraduate education.* Racine, Wisconsin: Johnson Foundation.

❀ ❀ ❀

## Transforming the Basic Course: Honors Public Speaking

*Catherine A. Dobris*
*Associate Professor of Communication*
*Indiana University-Purdue University Indianapolis*

In Beginning in Honors: A Handbook, Samuel Schuman (1995, 30) observes, that in times where universities may be pressured to cut costs and to "respond to student demands for vocational relevance . . . which is not conducive to curricular boldness and initiative," Honors courses may "open curricular doors otherwise barred, and can suggest directions which might otherwise be ruled out as costly or risky." He suggests that, "Honors Programs have an especially important role to play in restoring room for movement and contemplation in such an environment." Moreover, as Schuman illustrates, Honors courses tend to take one of four forms: 1) Honors sections of regular courses, 2) Enriched options within regular courses, 3) Special Honors courses, and 4) Honors projects. Whichever form Honors courses may take, there are a number of significant pedagogical concerns raised in the design, implementation and assessment of 100 level humanities courses. As one colleague in my Department asks frequently, "Is it bigger, better, more, deeper, or all of the above?"

A couple years ago I was asked by the Honors program and the Department of Communication Studies at IUPUI to develop an honors section of the basic public speaking course. I have taught it many times since. I provide a statement which addresses the question, "What makes it honors?" My public speaking course syllabus contains the following description:

> Compared to a regular section of this course, students will use a more advanced textbook, give longer speeches with increased research expectations, have more challenging assignments, do more informal and formal writing, use advanced technology, and engage in creative problem solving in the development and evaluation of speech-making.

**How is Honors different from an advanced course in the same subject area?**

In an advanced course it can be assumed that all students have mastered at least basic public speaking competencies learned in the lower level prerequisite. Since Honors Public Speaking has no prerequisite other than a 3.0 average, it cannot be assumed that students have learned even basic level skills in public speaking, such as, for example, outlining. Therefore, my assignments follow a similar pattern as those assigned in our multi-sectioned course, but with several significant distinctions in both breadth and depth.

**What makes a course worthy of "Honors" distinctions in the basic level course?** Specifically, in my public speaking class:

> ### "Is it bigger, better, more, deeper, or all of the above?"

Students will read, write and conduct research appropriate to a 100 level university course. If students have deficiencies in any of those areas they will take full responsibility to seek out appropriate assistance outside of the classroom to remedy those problems (e.g., The Writing Center, The Speaker=s Lab, mentoring, tutoring, as needed).

Students are expected to take careful notes on classroom lecture and discussion, to enhance the learning process throughout the course, even though there are no formal exams.

Students will do all readings on time and use those readings to execute all assignments in this course. There will, therefore, be no need to provide exams to ensure that students keep up on the readings. Most materials are not complex, however, students are expected to apply the readings to their own writing and speech-giving. The textbook for this section is somewhat more advanced and comprehensive than in the regular course.

Students will have the opportunity to provide more in-depth research and analysis than in a regular section of R110. There are fewer speeches which will allow for more preparation time, greater development of ideas, and longer speeches. There are also no exams, which provides more time for research and time for speaking in the classroom.

Students will have the opportunity to do more writing and more critical analysis of speeches, therefore enhancing their skills as public speakers and as effective consumers of communication.

Students will assume full responsibility of the course setting, to enhance the presentation of their last speech in the course. Students are encouraged to u for learning power point or some comparable software, outside se power point or some comparable software for earlier speeches as well, in order to get comfortable with the technology. Students may make appointments with The Speaker=s Lab for assistance with power point and other uses of technology for the classroom.

**What standard of comparison can we use between a regular course and an Honors section of that course? (e.g., Should student grading procedures be similar or different? Should student performances be assessed at a higher level?)**

I have found it useful so far, to use the same measures of assessment for basic competencies, however, I increase the number of areas they are assessed on and some of those areas require more advanced research and critical analysis. This is most evident in the final public speaking assignment in which students present a rhetorical criticism of a

contemporary speaker, drawing on materials from throughout the course as well as lectures on speech criticism.

**Conclusion**

So what makes it honors? In part it depends on the discipline and on the course. It is "bigger, better, more, deeper, *and* all of the above." The honors course is a wonderful opportunity for faculty to design course work that pushes beyond the usual boundaries of the class, for an audience that truly wants to be there. I=m not naive; every semester in our first day exercise students are asked why they are there and a good number of them reply, "because I needed at least one honors course this semester and this fit my schedule," or "to keep my honors scholarship." But whatever their initial motives, once in the classroom they live up to their moniker well and, with the instructor, help to create a rich, learning environment.

> **The honors course is a[n]... opportunity for faculty to design coursework that pushes beyond the usual boundaries.**

❋ ❋ ❋

## Hints for Adding Color to the Pedagogical Palette

*Brenda E. Knowles*
*Business & Economics*
*Indiana University South Bend*

### Preparing and Individualizing the Classroom Canvas

Those of us who have spent any time in a college classroom recognize the wisdom of Brophy and Good's (1996) conclusion that

> Elitist critics often undervalue teaching or even suggest that anyone can teach ('Those who can, do; those who can't, teach'). The data...refute

this myth.... Although it may be true that most adults could survive in the classroom, it is not true that most could teach effectively.... [Teachers] who do...these things successfully produce significantly more achievement than those who do not, but doing them successfully demands a blend of knowledge, energy, motivation, and communication and decision-making skills that many teachers, let alone ordinary adults, [lack]....

Seasoned teachers also acknowledge that the

Quality of teaching is directly contingent on the quality of the decision making that precedes the teaching. Decision making is a process...that integrates the various elements of teaching[:] ...establishing [the] classroom climate, planning for teaching, interacting with students, and evaluating performance and achievement.(Brophy and Good 1996, 3)

Simply put, the process of effective teaching involves a complex amalgam of disciplinary expertise and technical competency, knowledge of the most effective strategies as determined by the current research on learning theory, the ability to motivate students and oneself, and an appreciation of the dynamics of the group interactions that constitute the backdrop of a classroom climate that maximizes learning.

The following compendium of strategies derives from twenty-six years of teaching undergraduate and graduate business students. The primary rationale for implementing these techniques is to maximize students' involvement in the learning enterprise and thereby to add color to the classroom. The approaches delineated include exercises aimed at invigorating the classroom environment as well as facilitating interactive learning. While I can take credit for developing many of these activities, I have eagerly copied the ideas of my colleagues at Indiana University South Bend; those in FACET, Indiana University's Faculty Colloquium on Excellence in Teaching, a group from which I always derive inspiration and refreshment; and the presenters at the annual Master Teacher Symposium of the Academy of Legal Studies in Business, the premier professional organization for business law professors. Even though the passage of the years has obscured my ability to make individual attributions, I would be remiss if I failed to acknowledge the collective contributions of such gifted teachers to my own development.

Yet, those teachers from whom I have immensely benefitted bear out the observation that "teaching is, in the final analysis, a personal invention"(Kindsvatter 1996, 5). Moreover, pedagogy ". . . tends to be more suggestive than prescriptive. .

> **One can never reduce teaching to technique.**

. . Teachers will be most effective if they maintain their own personal identity and integrity while being guided by the tenets of pedagogy..."(Kindsvatter, Willen, and Ishler 1996, 5). Put differently, one can never reduce teaching to technique. Rather, as Parker J. Palmer (1998) rightly notes, "Good teaching comes from the identity and integrity of the teacher." I furthermore agree wholeheartedly with Palmer's assertion that

if students and subjects accounted for all the complexities of teaching,

104

our standard ways of coping would do—keep up with our fields as best we can and learn enough techniques to stay ahead of the student psyche. But there is another reason for these complexities: we teach who we are...(Palmer 1998, 2).

Hence, the classroom chromatics described herein, while they represent effective pedagogical techniques for me, will not work for everyone. Indeed,

> when we are unfaithful to the inward teacher and to the community of truth, we do lamentable damage to ourselves, to our students, and to the great things of the world that our knowledge holds in trust.... [But] the converse is equally true. [Authentic teachers bring] a blessing known to generations of students whose lives have been transformed by people who had the courage to teach—the courage to teach from the most truthful places in the landscape of self and world, the courage to invite students to discover, explore, and inhabit those places in the living of their own lives (Palmer 1998, 183).

## Making the Classroom Rosier

The genesis of a classroom climate that encourages students "to develop [the] motivation to learn as a general disposition..."(Brophy 1998, 172) represents an important adjunct of Palmer's notion of "the courage to teach." None of us needs to be reminded of the role the teacher's personality and his or her everyday behavior in the classroom plays in shaping student attitudes toward learning: We all can recount with great delight the impact of gifted teachers on our lives. In other words, "engagement in classroom activities tends to be high when students perceive their teacher is involved with them (liking them, responsive to their needs), but students tend to become disaffected when they do not perceive such involvement" (Brophy 1998, 22).

Thus classroom chromatics that fire up the students--exercises that ensure success in tincturing the classroom with a greater degree of motivation and effectuating an orientation that promotes autonomy in learning--are critical. Adding such hues means that the teacher must lay the foundations for making the classroom environment as inviting as possible, including reawaken[ing] a motivation system that may be barely operative when students enter their classrooms.... A related task is to refocus students' attention on understanding and developing their competencies and to diminish their concerns about external evaluation, especially grades.... In summary, the goal is to create an instructional program that capitalizes on students' intrinsic desires to learn, that focuses their attention on understanding and mastery, and that fosters academic values... (Brophy 1998, 25).

These suggestions for ensuring the success of any motivational efforts moreover illustrate the link between "compliance-gaining strategies" and teacher "immediacy"—such nonverbal signals as eye contact, smiling, or relaxed body language; and verbal manifestations such as humor, using personal examples (including "we" and "our" language), and vocal variety, as well as students' names (Brophy 1998, 25). In tandem, compliance-gaining strategies and immediacy can "reinforce each other to produce positive effects on motivation, especially in students who are not highly motivated at the beginning of the term" (Brophy 1998, 161-62).

## Orientations to Learning

A successful instructional program depends as well on a classroom environment that engenders students' confidence in their academic competencies and fosters high expectations for success with school tasks (Brophy 1998, 57). Numerous studies have touted the value of a teacher's reinforcing the self-efficacy perceptions of his or her students. Put differently, the effort and persistence needed to achieve flourish "when people possess a sense of efficacy or competence—that is, confidence that they have the ability (including the specific strategies needed) to succeed in the task if they choose to invest the necessary effort..."( Brophy 1998, 57).

To encourage the development of this characteristic, I give students materials early on provided to me by one of my School of Education colleagues, Dr. Randall Isaacson. This handout summarizes the current theories regarding the so-called "task/mastery" orientation to learning with its counterpart, the "ego/performance" orientation. I explain to students that although each person ordinarily possesses a combination of mastery and performance orientations, I will encourage a mastery orientation for goal achievement. We also discuss the characteristics of individuals who possess high- and low-efficacy so the students can gauge where they fall on this continuum. Throughout the semester, I refer to this handout as a reminder that adopting a mastery orientation will not only benefit them in this class but in all their courses.

## Summary of Critical Thinking Skills

Because the mastery orientation to learning focuses on improving skills and competencies, very early in the semester I provide students with a presentation on critical thinking that my Philosophy Department colleague, Dr. Lyle Zynda, has

prepared. I use these materials to acquaint the students with the concept of critical thinking in general; I then explain that legal analysis involves a specialized type of critical thinking (summarized by the mnemonic device, IDES, which stands for "Identify the legal issue, Define all the relevant terms, Enumerate the principles associated with the issue, and Show both sides" [plaintiff's and defendant's] using the facts) that I, in turn,

> **I have very high expectations for my students, and I communicate those expectations on a daily basis.**

discuss in a two-page handout. I use this IDES graphic virtually every day so as to communicate the most important objectives of the courses: the students' acquisition of the skill of legal analysis.

The educational research concerning "the effect of teacher expectations on student learning" is well documented and profound: teachers' views of the students' performance many times lead to self-fulfilling prophecies (Stipek 1998, 203). Accordingly, I have very high expectations for my students, and I communicate those expectations on a daily basis.

## Eradicating the Blues

Whatever strategies a teacher adopts in order to ensure student success, a teacher must remain aware of the fact that college instruction more closely resembles a marathon than a sprint. Hence, diminishing the wanness—or the blues—that can infuse classroom dynamics and maintaining the students' desire to learn entail

establishing a learning environment that creates a favorable context in which to socialize students' motivation to learn. These strategies involve helping students come to understand that classrooms are primarily places for learning and that acquiring knowledge and skills contributes to their quality of life (not just [to] their report card grades) (Brophy 1998, 168).

These endeavors require both inspiration and perseverance. Numerous researchers also have identified the need for "scaffolding" techniques as complements to motivational and metacognitive strategies, since "motivating students to learn requires not only bringing them to the lesson but bringing the lesson to them" (Stipek 1998, 50). Expert scaffolding, then, consists primarily of "assisting students at first by giving them reminders, directions, and hints, and then slowly withdrawing such assistance. The last step is to give students opportunities to apply and practice these strategies independently" (Stipek 1998, 50). Because each of the courses I teach has certain primary objectives—learning legal analysis, enhancing managerial problem-solving abilities, and enhancing communication skills—I spend a great deal of time implementing and reinforcing scaffolding strategies.

**Outlining the Text Chapters and Class Notes**

The first method I use—requiring the students to outline the chapters—may seem old fashioned. Over the years, I have increasingly experienced the vexing phenomenon of students' failing to read the text. Although I heavily augment the text with additional handouts (or "voices," as I call them) and materials that use the text as a springboard for exchanges of views, I expect students to read the book. In short, I view the book as the starting point for class discussions. However, I have of late noticed that many of the books remain in pristine condition throughout the semester. I have

always advocated outlining the material because outlining is the time-honored way of making sense of dense, complex, legal materials. In my early years, I made the outlines optional. My experience under this regime will undoubtedly sound familiar: only the high-performing students completed the outlines. About four years ago, in an attempt to reach the other, less gifted students, I began requiring the students to outline the book and their class notes. Once they do this, I then bring in examples of how they can turn the outline into smaller, note card-sized segments and thereby make the material more manageable. Since I cover about twenty-one chapters in the introduction to business law class, the students turn in one or two outlines per week. I comment on the outlines and suggest ways in which the students can more effectively organize the materials.

Once I give such guidance, they start to discern how to strengthen their organization of the materials. I typically have about twenty-five students in my class, and it takes surprisingly little time to glance over the outlines and make comments (the time spent grading therefore does not represent an insurmountable problem even in large classes). I have discovered that these outlines, in conjunction with the practice hypotheticals that I employ virtually every class period as a method for unifying the material, provide avenues for clarifying misconceptions and reinforcing deep—as opposed to rote—comprehension. Three times a semester (before every major exam), I review the outlines and give the students five points for each set of revised outlines (i.e., a maximum of 15 bonus points out of the 390 possible points). I constantly emphasize the need for revisions so that the outline can serve as the students' primary study vehicle—both in, and out, of class. This newly instituted regime, i.e., requiring the outlines and the subsequent revision of each, has had dramatic results: the overall grade point average for my classes has risen by about half a point (or more). Current students are much less resistant to doing the outlines than classes in the past were, in part, I believe, because these more recent class members can chart their own (upward) progress. Outlining therefore has evolved into a worthwhile learning activity, the value of which the students appreciate.

Since motivating students to learn requires a goal-oriented approach that "develops key knowledge and skills in ways that support understanding, appreciation, and life applications" (Brophy 1998, 174), I believe I have, through the implementation of this activity, increased the students' metacognitive awareness and cemented their control of their own learning strategies. Indeed, "instructional strategists have shown that learners retain more information when their learning is goal directed and structured around key concepts"(Brophy 1998, 185). I therefore relentlessly pursue activities that necessitate the students' processing and applying the course's content.

## Student-Generated Transparencies

While the "minute papers" that have become a well-recognized vehicle for identifying student questions and concerns represent a rather simple technique for enhancing metacognition, students' comprehension of the material increases in a climate in which the teacher introduces a cognitive strategy, explains its usefulness, models the particular strategy while engaging the students in guided practice, and (lastly) reflects on how well the students have accomplished the activity's primary goals (Brophy 1998, 185). An exercise that

reinforces this progression and that has been very instrumental in student learning consists of the students' creating transparencies that either summarize a given concept or that answer a hypothetical. I introduce this technique, which I learned from my School of Business and Economics colleague, Dr. Paul Kochanowski, about midway through the semester after I have shared numerous of my own transparencies/slides with the students. This in-class project takes about 20 minutes but is well worth the class time.

I first break the class into groups of four or five and ask them to put themselves in the shoes of the teacher and then develop a transparency (or slide) that analyzes a hypothetical or that explains a given concept—say "defamation." I also have used this same activity in asking the students to prepare a graphic that extends student learning—say a comparison of the common law rules concerning the sale of goods with those of the Uniform Commercial Code and the Convention on Contracts for the International Sale of Goods. Any time I use this method—and I do so about three times a semester—the students show a substantially heightened understanding of the material. I attribute this success to the value of group/collaborative work (Kindsvatter 1996, 295); the intellectual jolt the students receive from changing roles with me, the teacher; and the cognitive benefits derived from the reverse-engineering in which they have engaged. They come away from this exercise with a demonstrably enlarged appreciation of how to approach both the exam/quiz hypotheticals (all of which are taken from real-life cases and scenarios) and the issues they will encounter in the legal environment in which they live and work. Each group critiques the work product of

> It is vital that we find...strategies for keeping our own motivational levels high.

the others, so this is an opportunity for the students to practice self-evaluation, a skill that, in my experience, most students have developed only nascently. Furthermore, the discussion of the transparencies provides the students with "opportunities to assess their performance and to correct and learn from their mistakes"(Brophy 1998, 193) thereby reinforcing a mastery orientation to learning. This exercise also permits me to "include a post-activity debriefing or reflection that reemphasizes the activity's purpose and goals, reflects on how (and how well) [these] have been accomplished, and reminds [the] students about where the activity fits within the larger unit or curriculum strand"( Brophy 1998, 193). This involvement by the class members replaces the monochromatism derived from the teacher's undue involvement in, and control over, the classroom with the variegated colors that result from relinquishing control and ceding additional authority and responsibility to the students.

## Conclusion

I wholeheartedly agree with the assertion that "the quality of student learning is directly, although not exclusively, related to the quality of teaching. Therefore, one of the most promising ways to improve learning is to improve teaching" (Angelo 1993, 7). Because the hurly-burly of academic life can exhaust and enervate us, it is vital that we find ways of adding color to the teaching enterprise, including strategies for keeping our own motivational levels high. Each of us is the artist of a decidedly individualized canvas. It is my hope that the suggestions I have made will generate new hues or tints in our respective palettes. Whatever style emerges, I hope that we see our time in front of the academic easel as an opportunity to "enter, not evade, the tangles of teaching so that we can understand them better and negotiate them with more grace, not only to

guard our own spirits but also to serve our students well" (Palmer 1998, 7).

**References:**

Angelo, Thomas A. And K. Patricia Cross. 1993. *Classroom assessment techniques: A handbook for college teachers*, 2d ed. San Francisco: Jossey-Bass.

Brophy, Jere E. and Thomas L. Good. 1996. Research in early childhood and / elementary school teaching programs, 3d ed. In *Dynamics of effective teaching,* ed. Richard Kindsvatter, William Willen, and Margaret Ishler. White Plains, New York: Longman.

Brophy, Jere E. 1998. *Motivating students to learn*. Boston: McGraw-Hill.

Kindsvatter, Richard, William Willen, and Margaret Ishler. 1996. *Dynamics of effective teaching*, 3d ed. Wite Plains, New York: Longman.

Palmer, Parker J. 1998. *The courage to teach : Exploring the inner landscape of a teacher's life*. San Francisco, Calif. : Jossey-Bass.

Stipek, Deborah. 1998. *Motivation to learn : From theory to practice*, 3d ed. Boston: Allyn and Bacon.

❋ ❋ ❋

## In-class Writing to Advance Critical Thinking

*Elaine Roth*
*English*
*Indiana University South Bend*

When I teach composition, I regularly use a terrific in-class writing assignment that advances critical thinking. (I lifted this exercise from one of my graduate school professors, Jim Crosswhite.) About halfway through the semester, once students feel fairly comfortable developing an argumentative thesis for an expository essay, I ask them to take out a piece of paper and write their thesis at the top. Then I ask them to write several paragraphs in the voice of someone who opposes this position, explaining this person's perspective. However, their opponent can't simply be a straw man who demonstrates his stupidity for holding beliefs contrary to the student's. Instead, this voice of opposition must come from someone the student respects and admires.

First the students write in the voice of their opposition, explaining their commitment to this position that opposes the student's thesis. Then, in another paragraph or two, students describe their opponent, painting a picture of the kind of person who might hold this contrary position, from the clothes this opponent might wear to the type of car he might drive. The result suggests the cultural contexts that produce different points of view.

The creation of this sympathetic opponent reveals the value of critically regarding a topic from more than one perspective. Rather than asserting that anyone who could think other than they do must be beyond regard, students writing in the voice of the sympathetic opponent encounter the legitimacy of varying opinions. Invariably,

> **Students writing in the voice of the sympathetic opponent encounter the legitimacy of varying opinions.**

at least one student will change her thesis and actually adopt the position of her former opponent by the end of the exercise! This exercise raises a number of topics for discussion, from the range of beliefs that surround a single topic, to the stereotypes associated with particular belief systems. In addition, it rewards different types of student writing, including argumentative writing and creative writing.

❅ ❅ ❅

## Demonstrating Computer Applications

*Rosanne M. Cordell*
*Franklin D. Schurz Library*
*Indiana University South Bend*

When I demonstrate new software for students in a computer lab, I ask for a volunteer to keyboard on the demo computer. When a student is working on the computer that is projected for the class to follow, it forces me to be explicit in my instructions, and it frees me to walk around the lab to give individual help. Since the student on the demo computer is bound to make at least one of the common errors made with the particular software, it also allows me to give instructions in correcting errors as a natural part of the demonstration. Students keep up with each other much more easily than with an experienced software user, they seem to feel more relaxed about the whole lesson, and I am able to respond to questions without

110

a computer creating physical distance between the class and me. Of course, I thank the student keyboarder profusely, and have even been known to give a candy treat to the volunteer!

> **Good pedagogy... encourages a sense of shared-experience.**

Active learning and cooperative learning are combined when students learn from each other in hands-on situations. Such pedagogy allows students to retain a much greater percent of class material. Good pedagogy also encourages a sense of shared-experience and sense of humor regarding the natural errors we all make as new learners. When teaching course material that requires a different set of skills than those mastered for traditional learning situations, the instructor must remember that students will have far less confidence in their ability to master the material. Software use and database searching are teachable skills, but instructors may find that a collaborative atmosphere is more conducive to learning than attempting to adapt traditional lecture techniques.

### References:

Hunt, Nancy P. and Roy M. Bohlin. 1995. Events and practices that promote attitudes and emotions in computing courses. *Journal of Computing in Teaching Education* 11, no. 3 (Spring): 21-2.

Kember, David. 2000. *Action learning and action research: Improving the quality of teaching and learning.* London: Kogan Page.

Margrath, William. 2001. A Return to Interactivity: The Third Wave in Educational Uses of Information Technology. *CALICO Journal* 18, no. 2: 283-94.

Silberman, Melvin L. 1996. *Active learning: 101 strategies to teach any subject.* Boston: Allyn and Bacon.

❋ ❋ ❋

## Praxis Paper: Theorizing Practice in Interpersonal Communication

*Stuart Schrader*
*Communication*
*Indiana University-Purdue University Indianapolis*

### Background

This paper is distributed to students as their second of two papers in an Interpersonal Communication course. Over 1,000 students a year take this as the eleventh largest gateway course at IUPUI. Interpersonal Communication is a semi-standardized course in which nearly 50% is systematically crafted by the faculty who teach the course and the remainder is contextualized by the specific instructor.

The course asks students to consider communication as a collaborative relational process. Ultimately students focus on how communication is at the center of listening, creation and presentation of selves, perception, spoken language, nonverbal cues, relational development, maintenance and termination, managing conflict, and culture. When a student completes this course he or she should have a greater competency in appreciating, recognizing and applying interpersonal communication practices and processes in culturally contextualized conversations.

Students often begin with a mixed amount of enthusiasm for the course depending on their reason for enrolling; however, most students usually become highly engaged in interpersonal communication courses one third of the way into the course. Students at this point realize that the communication concepts being presented and the classroom stories being shared are leading to more reflexive moments in their interpersonal relationships. One of the central reasons for this turn toward greater self-learning is because of praxis-oriented exercises, activities, and paper assignments.

## Pedagogical Move: Rationale for Exploring Interpersonal Communication Dialogue in Everyday Social Encounter

Praxis can be viewed, according to Lang, Little and Cronen (1990, 41), from an Aristotelian perspective as "what free persons do together in a community that makes for a way of life." This view highlights the core element of transferability from theory to practice, yet, also recognizes that not all people are free to engage in such activities. Therefore, systemic inquiry into applied social communicative practice requires an emphasis in exploring real life situations (Petronio 1999). These scenarios are riddled with contextual communicative situations in which racial, ethnic, gender, sexual orientation and other social inequities are commonly found. In order to systemically foster praxis, it is essential to emphasize to students the importance of how power relationships are developed, reinforced, influenced and ultimately played out in communication contexts (Crawford 1988). Students learn how to better understand the struggle for power within interpersonal conversations and that the "mechanism by which power is exercised consists of our being excluded from participation in the speech acts that define our lives or of our being compelled to participate in speech acts that injure or offend us" (Pearce 1994, 145).

## Student Outcomes

Therefore, students are asked to develop an applied dialogue paper that assists them in

viewing relational conversations from both a "third person objective perspective," and a "first person subjective perspective. According to Pearce (1994, 22) shifting perspectives is a "persistent remind[er] that what we say and do 'about' interpersonal communication is at the same time, inevitably, also taking a turn in interpersonal communication."

Students appreciate the opportunity to engage with others about how inequities in given sequences of speech acts are due in part to racial, ethnic, gender, sexual orientation, disabilities or other diversity related issues. Students remark that they viewed theory in action when recognizing how some participants' voices in this assignment are more often privileged, stressed, and/or emphasized due, in part, to differences in cultural boundaries (Pearce 1994).

### Paper Requirements
-5 pages in length (page minimum)
-At least three outside academic sources cited in the paper
-Within the paper include at least 5 concepts from our course and highlight them
-Work cited page (MLA or APA citation style)

### Assignment Procedure
Please explore an interpersonal dialogue with one other person. The other person can be a friend, family member, partner, co-worker or a mixture of these roles. In your paper briefly outline her/his relational role in relationship to your own. Ask the other person permission to audio tape your conversation. Audio tape a conversation and discuss the issue of relational responsibility. Engage in talk about their feelings, perspective, and outlook on whether or not people should be relationally responsible to

each other. Let the other person define what this means prior to giving any further explanations.

## Questions to Ask During Your Interview

After they have shared, please ask the following questions:

(1) Do you feel that people should try to be consistently respectful, honest, connected, mindful, and open with all people?

(2) Do you feel that relational responsibility as you have defined it should be practiced equally with friends, family members, peers, and all others that one has close contact with in one's life?

(3) Should one extend this relational responsibility to everyone?

(4) How does the intersection of gender, culture, and race/ethnicity play a role in this type of practice?

(5) What role does power play in this form of interaction? Who is privileged and who is muted in certain conversations? How does one become disenfranchised in a conversation?

## Have a 10-15 minute conversation that centers on these issues.

## Closing and Reviewing Your Interview

When you are done thank the interviewee for their involvement. Write notes to yourself at this point about your conversation and try to note your interviewee's verbal and nonverbal reactions while engaging in this conversation. Playback your

audio-tape and transcribe (type up) in a dialogue format a brief 1-2 page segment of the material that seems most relevant to your paper's main points. Try to select the most important segment of the conversation (it might help to jump ahead and think about the thesis statement for your paper at this point).

## Advice in Writing Your Paper

First, write a thesis statement that reflects issues we have addressed in the following sections of the course: (1) relational process, (2) friendships, and (3) intimate relations. Select five concepts from one or several of these sections that you wish to address in your paper. Craft a thesis statement that integrates both your selection of concepts and your selection of three outside academic articles. Choose articles that assist and guide you in framing your paper. Again, please refer to the bibliography section on the web site or go to *CommIndex* for assistance in finding related articles. Second, create an introduction with a clever opening statement, a single-sentence thesis statement and a set of 2-3 main points. Third, blend, weave and integrate your five concepts, your three articles, and the analysis of your conversation into one cohesive body of work. Use full explanations for the concepts and integrate information from your articles to critically examine your entire conversation. Use excerpts from your transcripts to help in your analysis and integrate this into your work. Lastly, create a review in your conclusion and a summative analysis for your closing.

**References:**

Crawford, B. 1988. Women and communicative power: *A conceptual approach to communication strategies.* In *Women and communicative power: Theory, research and practice,* ed. Carol A. Valentine and Nancy Hoar. Annandale, Virginia: Speech Communication Association.

Lang, P., M. Little,, and V. Cronen. 1990. The systemic professional domains of action and the question of neutrality. *Human Systems: The Journal of Systemic Consultation and Management* 1: 39-55.

Pearce, W. Barnett. 1994. *Interpersonal communication: Making social worlds.* New York: Harper Collins Press.

Petronio, S. 1999. "Translating scholarship into practice": An alternative metaphor. *Journal of Applied Communication* 27: 87-91.

❋ ❋ ❋

# From "Mistakes" to "Mastery"
*Elizabeth Goering*
*Communication*
*Indiana University-Purdue University Indianapolis*

My creative writing teacher in high school once told us, "If you want to become an excellent writer, making mistakes is the second smartest thing you can do." She paused a moment, knowing we were all wondering what the smartest thing we could do might be, and then added, "The smartest thing you can do is to learn to recognize mistakes others have made before you make them yourself." I have found this mentor/teacher's wisdom useful throughout my twenty-plus years of teaching, first at the high school level and later at the university. Implicit in my teacher's observation is the recognition that we all make mistakes—even, perhaps, permission to make them—as well as the realization that mistakes can be transformed into learning opportunities.

An activity I would like to share with new faculty that is born from this philosophy of learning is an in-class exercise I call "Good Speech, Bad Speech." I use this activity to introduce a unit on effective public speaking in an introductory communication course. Although the exercise, as described here, is specific to communication, I believe the underlying assumptions about transforming "mistakes" to "mastery" as well as the general design of the activity could be adapted to many other skills, courses, and disciplines.

I begin the "Good Speech, Bad Speech" activity by dividing the class into small groups of four to six people. Then I ask the students to think of poor speeches they have heard in the past. I prime their thinking with prompts, such as "maybe it was a sermon, or a professor's lecture, or perhaps a speech given by a fellow student." After giving the students a minute or two to think of examples, I ask them to brainstorm in their groups, identifying specific things that made those speeches so poor. In other words, I ask them to pinpoint the "mistakes" the speakers made.

> **Mistakes can be transformed into learning opportunities.**

When all of the groups have a fairly lengthy list of "mistakes" they have seen other people make in giving speeches, I ask each group to prepare a speech that demonstrates a few of these errors. After

114

a volunteer from each group performs his/her group's speech for the class, we analyze the presentations and process the activity. We begin by identifying the specific mistakes illustrated by the speakers. During the analysis of the speeches, I make an effort to provide students with a theory-based framework for understanding the mistakes illustrated in terms of both the structure/content of the speech and its presentation/delivery. Finally we discuss ways to transform those mistakes into mastery of public speaking. I have found this activity to be an effective way to introduce the unit on public speaking for several reasons:

**Many students truly are apprehensive about public speaking**, and this activity makes it feel "safer" for them. The students don't need to worry about doing poorly or making mistakes—they're supposed to. And then they're given an opportunity to learn from those mistakes.

**The activity builds on the assumption that students often intuitively know what works** or doesn't work in public speaking. The exercise helps students realize that, and the subsequent discussion processing the activity provides them with a framework for theorizing what they know.

Perhaps most important, **the activity reinforces the notion that the analysis of our own mistakes as well as the mistakes of others can be a springboard to mastery.**

Brainstorming is a strategy I often use in my classes, and over the years I have identified some ways to make brainstorming work better. One could say, that I myself have "learned from previous mistakes." Here are some suggestions that have worked in my classroom:

**"Teach" students how to brainstorm effectively**; don't just assume they know how to do it. I establish communication rules related to brainstorming, such as "write down every idea that is generated" or "don't discuss ideas until the brainstorming session is over."

If students appear apprehensive about sharing ideas, which sometimes is the case early in a semester, I will **try to establish a climate that encourages creative thinking and free expression** by having the students brainstorm on a fantasy topic, such as "imagine what the world would be like if we all had eyes on our thumbs instead of on our faces." The two minutes spent off topic is typically time well spent, because it helps produce a climate that enhances future brainstorming.

During the brainstorming session, I often will **offer "prompts"** that are designed to help the students think about the problem or topic in new and creative ways. For example, for this exercise, after letting students brainstorm without constraints for a minute or so, I might suggest that they think about things the speaker did, and after a short while, I will suggest that they focus on problems with the speech itself.

❋ ❋ ❋

# Chapter 7:

# Keeping Track

*You are continually making and revising decisions about teaching and learning.*

*Sharon Hamilton*

# How Do I Get Started on a Teaching Portfolio?

*Jay R. Howard*
*Sociology*
*Indiana University-Purdue University Columbus*

Teaching portfolios are now common enough that you've likely heard of their utility in the demonstration and assessment of effective teaching. But just what is a teaching portfolio and what should go into one? How does one get started collecting materials for a portfolio?

A teaching portfolio is a collection of materials that allows one to document teaching performance over time. Portfolios allow one to highlight what it is one does well as a teacher. Most commonly the materials are arranged in a three-ring binder. The length of the portfolio depends on the purpose and audience (e.g., teaching award, promotion and tenure, job application). There is no single "correct" list of categories or sections for portfolios, but the following eight elements are commonly included in portfolios. The important thing is to begin collecting materials for your portfolio early in your career to make the construction of the portfolio easier and more comprehensive. A good way to being is to get a set of file folders, label them with the eight categories listed below, and keep them handy for collecting appropriate materials.

> **Begin collecting materials for your portfolio early in your career.**

## Statement of Teaching Philosophy

The most important component of the teaching portfolio is the statement of teaching philosophy, sometimes referred to as a reflective statement on teaching. Whatever other materials or evidence are presented in the portfolio, they should support the claims being made in the statement of teaching philosophy. The candidate should ask him/herself, "What are my goals in teaching and what is it in my teaching that I do especially well?" Ideally, you should be able to identify a small number (around three) aspects of your teaching that you wish to highlight in your reflective statement. Perhaps you are an outstanding lecturer who effectively engages students by drawing them into your explanation of the material. Maybe your strength is facilitating discussions – being unafraid to release control of the class. Spurring students toward critical thinking or excelling at utilization of technology to promote greater student learning might be your strongest skill. Developing mentoring relationships with students may be what makes you an outstanding teacher. Whatever it is that makes your teaching effective should be clearly profiled in the statement of teaching philosophy, making reference to the types of evidence that support your claims found in other sections of the portfolio.

Having served on multiple teaching award and hiring committees, it is clear to me that the statement of philosophy will most likely be carefully read. The rest of the portfolio may not be as carefully read, so it is crucial to make and support your central claims in the statement of teaching philosophy.

## List of Courses Taught

Depending upon the purpose of the portfolio, it is often good idea to include a complete list of courses taught by semester, including the number of students in each class. If the portfolio is being used as one piece of information in a job application, this material may be especially important. The hiring department wants to know exactly which courses were taught, when and where, and with what number of students in the class. Often this information is not clearly included in a curriculum vitae. Nonetheless, it might be crucial information for a hiring department. For teaching awards or promotion and tenure decisions, a clear record of the courses taught may be required as well.

### Student Evaluations and Comments

Giving a committee all of the course evaluations you have received over a period of years is rather like sending the raw data you collected to a journal for review. No reviewer wants to read through all of your course evaluations - though they may ask for a random sample of complete evaluations from a small number of courses. Instead, you should summarize what you have learned about your teaching from your evaluations. Ask yourself which of the quantitative measures on the evaluation form best assess the claims you make about in your statement of teaching philosophy. If I have claimed that I excel at teaching critical thinking, there is likely a measure included on the evaluation form such as "My instructor stimulates my thinking." Create a table that shows your scores over time on this item on your course evaluations. Can you demonstrate consistently high scores? Can you demonstrate improvement over time? Perhaps you can show that your scores were consistently above the 75th percentile for all instructors in your department or on campus.

Given the increasing emphasis on student learning found in higher education today, all instructors should consider reporting the course evaluation measure of student learning (e.g., "My instructor helped me learn a lot in this course."). Can you demonstrate that students consistently report that they perceive they are learning in your courses?

Likewise the qualitative comments that accompany the quantitative evaluations can show support for the claims you make about your teaching in your statement. As noted above, a committee may request/require a random sample of complete evaluations (both quantitative scores and qualitative comments). However, you can also report comments that specifically address the claims you make. Using critical thinking as an example once again, you can report comments related to this issue over multiple semesters and multiple courses. For example, "I enjoyed the challenge to think beyond the material given." Use comments to demonstrate a repeated pattern of student comments on your strengths and how they are related to learning ("The material that is taught is challenging, but the instructor does a good job with helping each student learn.") Typically, a page or two of student comments is sufficient to make the point. While selected comments, because they are selected, may not be weighed as heavily as other forms of evidence, they are one more indicator of teaching effectiveness that can support the claims you make about yourself in the statement of teaching philosophy.

### Peer Evaluations

It is important to include peer reviews of your teaching in your portfolio. At a minimum, this involves an observation of a single session of a class you teach. The reviewer writes comments addressing your strengths and areas for potential growth as an instructor. Ideally, the reviewer also assesses the course materials (choice of text, exams, assignments, level of rigor, etc.) to present a more well-rounded perspective of your teaching. A colleague in your discipline who is known as an advocate of quality teaching is the ideal peer reviewer. In cases where this is not possible, campus centers for teaching and learning often have staff that is trained to conduct peer reviews. While they may not be able to address specific content issues, they can address your teaching methodologies. Often hiring, promotion and tenure, and award committees want to hear from someone who has actually seen you teach and can talk about your teaching from firsthand observation!

## Presentations, Publications and Research on Teaching

When you present your research at professional meetings, consider presenting your teaching materials as well. Often there are sessions dedicated to teaching. Consider submitting an abstract or volunteer to organize a session on the teaching of your specialty area. Also be on the lookout for opportunities to publish your teaching ideas in disciplinary specific outlets (such as *Teaching Sociology*, *Communication Education*, or *Teaching of Psychology*) or an interdisciplinary outlet (such as *College Teaching*). Your disciplinary association may also publish teaching related materials which could serve as an outlet for you.

## Professional and Community Service Related to Teaching

Another category to keep track of is the service you do that is related to teaching. Service on a teaching committee on your campus or within a professional organization is an example. Reviewing articles or books for a teaching journal is another example. This type of activity also has the added benefit of placing you within a professional network of people who value and affirm teaching in higher education. Likewise, they may be potential external reviewers for the promotion and tenure process.

Activities in the community where you share your expertise with others can be service related to teaching. Being invited to your child's third grade class to talk about the scientific method or visiting a high school literature class to present your research are examples of extending your teaching beyond the walls of your classroom.

## Professional Development

For your teaching portfolio, keep a listing of all the workshops and seminars related to teaching that you attend. Often at professional meetings, there are sessions on teaching. These can be a wonderful source of new ideas and reinvigoration for teaching excellence. While attendance at such events by itself won't get you promotion and tenure, it does demonstrate your commitment to continued improvement as a teacher.

## Examples of Student Work

Student work is a somewhat tricky category for a portfolio. We all have students who were excellent before they ever entered our classrooms. It is easy to take the work of your best students and claim they do well because they were in your course. However, it is not a very convincing argument. Instead, look for assignments that challenge students to higher order thinking in your courses or challenge students to integrate a range of material. Show how your assignments lead to student work that achieves the desired learning goal. If you can show a single student's improvement over time, it makes a compelling argument for successful teaching. Remember to seek the student's permission before including their work in your teaching portfolio.

> **This type of activity...plac[es] you within a professional network of people who value and affirm teaching in higher education.**

## Conclusion

No two portfolios should look exactly alike. Even a single person's portfolio should be revised and reordered depending upon the audience. If a promotion and tenure committee wants materials grouped in certain categories, arrange the portfolio accordingly. If a teaching award lists six or seven criteria for the award, consider rearranging your portfolio according to the criteria specified. It is often a good idea to begin each section of the portfolio with a very brief introduction that outlines the contents of the section and their purpose for inclusion in the portfolio. You always want to make a portfolio easy to read and materials easy to find.

## References:

Chism, Nancy Van Note. 1999. *Peer review of teaching : A sourcebook.* Bolton, Massachusetts: Anker.

Edgerton, Russell, Pat Hutchings, and Kathleen Quinlan. 1991. *The teaching portfolio: Capturing the scholarship in teaching.* Washington, D.C.: American Association for Higher Education.

Rieman, Patricia L. 2000. *Teaching portfolios: Presenting your professional best.* Boston: McGraw Hill.

Seldin, Peter. 1993. *Successful Use of Teaching Portfolios.* Bolton, Massachusetts: Anker.

❊ ❊ ❊

## Course Notebooks

*S. Holly Stocking*
*Journalism*
*Indiana University Bloomington*

I used to keep my course notes, including lecture notes, in files. That was fine, except that things fell out of the files as I carried them from classroom to home and back again. Then one semester I saw a colleague pull out a three-ring binder. It was her course notebook. In it she kept everything for the course – the roster at the front, followed by the syllabus, and then her lecture notes. It was so convenient! The grade book could go in the front pocket, and any papers the students turned in could go in the back. In the years since, I've taken to using post-it notes to mark each section of the notebook, with one note marked "today" for the day's lecture, and another for "syllabus" for that day's section of the syllabus. As I move from one day to the next, I just move the post-it note. A simple thing, but it's really helped to keep me organized and my carrying case tidy. Students are more likely now to remark that I look organized, too -- a nice side-benefit I never expected.

❊ ❊ ❊

## Getting Started on a Teaching Portfolio

*Sharon Hamilton*
*English*
*Indiana University Purdue University Indianapolis*

### What is a Teaching Portfolio?

Long before you enter your first classroom as an instructor, you make many important teaching decisions. As soon as you cross the threshold of your first classroom, you begin to modify those decisions. As your students bring their array of perspectives, questions, and concerns to your classes, you make even more changes, and when you read your evaluations at the end of your first semester, you may even consider starting all over again from scratch, making sweeping changes. Or you might be strongly affirmed that most of what you have done in your course is valuable and beneficial to students, but you still need or want to make some adjustments in a few areas. The significant constant is that you are continually making and revising decisions about teaching and learning, through any given class session, any semester, and any year of teaching. Over time, these changes signal development, improvement, and increasing sophistication in understanding how to help students learn more effectively.

A teaching portfolio captures key moments in this arc of change, improvement, and increasing sophistication. It makes visible the doubts, the questions, the uncertainties, the decisions, and the successes on your path to achieving excellence in teaching. It also makes visible the missteps along the way to achieving your teaching goals, and how you use what you discover along the paths of these missteps to find a better pathway to improve student learning.

The words "collection, selection, reflection, evaluation, and projection" are often used to encapsulate the basic structure of a teaching portfolio, in order to provide a framework for making the invisible work of teaching visible – to oneself as well as to others. In order to collect, select, reflect, evaluate, and project, you need first of all to focus and organize. You need some kind of conceptual framework, or you will simply amass so much material that it will overwhelm

rather than guide you, and it will similarly overwhelm anyone who reads your portfolio. This takes us directly the notion of purpose: Why are you creating your portfolio? What do you want it to achieve for you?

## Why Begin a Portfolio?

Portfolios may serve many functions. The clearer you are on your goal for your portfolio, the more it will likely benefit you. Some possible functions for portfolios include the following:

Improving your teaching – or some particular aspect of your teaching, such as motivating students, assessing student learning, creating more effective assignments;

Improving student learning, which seems similar to the above, but actually you will find that the different focus will yield different kinds of documentation and reflection;

Preparing for promotion and tenure

Applying for an award or a new position.

If you are a beginning faculty member, you should limit your goal and focus to one particular aspect of improving teaching or learning. Take the aspect of teaching/learning that most worries you, and make it your goal to improve in that area. Let's suppose you are concerned about grading students effectively, so that they learn from your grading. You might fear you are being too harsh or too easy, or that students do not pay sufficient attention to your guidance.

> **Excellence in teaching involves... analyzing and examining teaching and learning, determining areas for improvement, systematically taking steps for improvement, and evaluating your improvement.**

123

Begin by writing down your goal. Let's say it is something like the following: I want to improve my grading of student work so that students benefit from my comments, and use my comments to improve their work in this course.

Then write down all the related issues, such as concern about inflated grades, or harsh grades, or fair grades, or whether your grading matches your learning objectives, or whether your grading, learning objectives, assignments, course work, and classroom activities are all in alignment. If possible, word them as questions.

Determine what kinds of evidence would provide support for your questions, and begin to collect your evidence during your first semester. Reflect upon and analyze your evidence throughout the semester, and make (and keep track of) any adjustments necessary. You might consider the following:

Student comments when you hand back graded work
Students' work on subsequent assignments
Student evaluations at the end of the semester
Student evaluations mid-semester
And so on…

At the end of your first semester, analyze your overall semester's work on grading (or whatever you decide to focus on) and determine what you might change. Try out these changes the second semester, and use similar sources of evidence for comparison.

While this will capture only one small part of your teaching, consider how much you could improve your teaching and/ or student learning over a five year period, with a different focus each year. Starting small does not preclude moving into ever expanding areas.

By the time you are ready for promotion or tenure, you will have a wealth of data to make a case for excellence in teaching. One common misconception is equating excellence with perfection. Excellence in teaching involves, among other things, analyzing and examining teaching and learning, determining areas for improvement, systematically taking steps for improvement, and evaluating your improvement. Evidence of growth and improvement, put together selectively from your focused portfolios, may provide a compelling argument as you assemble a more comprehensive portfolio for promotion and tenure or for a teaching award.

## Moving from Portfolio to SoTL

If you follow the above guidelines for beginning and expanding your portfolio, you will be engaged in what is often called "scholarly teaching." It is easily adapted to the scholarship of teaching. If you use your focused area of concern as a site for inquiry, familiarize yourself with the literature and the national conversations in that area of inquiry, take a systematic approach to exploring your area of inquiry, and disseminate your findings in a public forum through presentation or publication, you are moving into the realm of the scholarship of teaching and learning. But merely the doing is not sufficient, either for an effective focused portfolio or for the scholarship of teaching and learning. Scholarly teaching requires reflection, evaluation, and projection for future learning situations. The scholarship of teaching and learning takes that a step further, and requires a systematic exploration and public dissemination.

❋ ❋ ❋

# Annual Report Preparation

*Katherine L. Jackson*
*Business & Economics*
*Indiana University South Bend*

Does the preparation of your annual report seem daunting? Few relish that beginning-of-the-year task and yet so much of our livelihood depends on its accurate and complete construction. In the past as the deadline loomed, I would begin the yearly scramble to find those pieces of paper that would remind me what I did over the last year. Then followed the obligatory office cleaning. All too often I ended up with a document entitled *Things I Wish I had put in My Annual Report.* I was, on occasion, my own worst enemy as I would forego salary increases simply because I had forgotten that I served on this or that committee, presented a paper at conference X, or had given a speech to group Y. At the time of the event I was sure I would never forget, but invariably with all that goes on over a year I did forget and sometimes I forgot huge events or really spectacular things I had accomplished. I was in desperate need of a system.

I decided to employ an old trick. I thought to myself, If my best friend came to me with this problem, what would I advise him or her?" At first I envisioned a system where my friend would write her annual report in weekly sections where she would recap each week's events into tidy capsules. Yeah, and we all have time for that. So my elaborate system was out. What about a simple folder/calendar system? This would be quick to set up, easy to use and, most of all one that she would not abandon six months down the road. I spent five whole minutes setting up my new system. I made up three file folders – one for teaching, one for research and one more for service. I put them in a spiral file holder on my desktop. I have also used a drawer that I shoved everything into, but the papers were pretty mashed. Use whatever works for you. I then put everything that I did such as announcements, conference programs, and positive feedback from colleagues or students into the appropriate folder. I put letters asking me to serve on committees into the folder, student evaluations; well you can see the list goes on.

> **So much of our livelihood depends on [the annual report's] accurate and complete construction.**

The other prong in my attack was to hang on to my appointment books. I have a paperbased appointment book (although one could easily adjust for a computer-based appointment calendar) and when I write in a meeting, I note the meeting and its tentative length. I do this because my dean wants to know not only what committees I serve on, but how much work they are and one way to show that is by how often the particular committee meets and for how long. I put copies of finished committee reports in my folders so I can recall how much outside time I spent preparing documents. Then when annual report time rolls around I close my office door, go through my folder and calendar, and make a list of everything I did over the last year. This list is always impressive and makes me feel good right at the start of preparing the report. I then have something to use as a checklist as I prepare my annual report. I have since gone down to one file folder (I am really lazy), but then I have to sort it at the end, so use whichever system works for you.

❋ ❋ ❋

# Contributors

Gretchen L. Anderson
Associate Professor of Chemistry
Indiana University South Bend
ganderso@iusb.edu

Rick Aniskiewicz
Professor of Sociology
Indiana University Kokomo
raniskie@iuk.edu

Pat Ashton
Associate Professor of Sociology
Indiana University-Purdue University Fort Wayne
ashton@ipfw.edu

Kevin Sue Bailey
Professor of Education
Indiana University Southeast
kbailey@ius.edu

Charles Barman
Professor of Education
Indiana University-Purdue University Indianapolis
cbarman@iupui.edu

Doug Barney
Professor of Business Administration
Indiana University Southeast
dbarney@ius.edu

Angela H. Becker
Associate Professor of Psychology
Indiana University Kokomo
abecker@iuk.edu

Erv Boschman
Professor of Chemistry
Indiana University-Purdue University Indianapolis
erv@iu.edu

Sharon K. Calhoon
Associate Professor of Psychology
Indiana University Kokomo
scalhoon@iuk.edu

Valerie N. Chang
Professor of Social Work
Indiana University-Purdue University Indianapolis
vchang@iupui.edu

Louise Collins
Associate Professor of Philosophy
Indiana University South Bend
loucolli@iusb.edu

Rosanne M. Cordell
Associate Librarian
Indiana University South Bend
rcordell@iusb.edu

Donna J. Dahlgren
Associate Professor of Psychology
Indiana University Southeast
ddahlgre@ius.edu

Catherine A. Dobris
Associate Professor of Communication Studies
Indiana University-Purdue University Indianapolis
cdobris@iupui.edu

Kathryn Ernstberger
Associate Professor of Business Administration
Indiana University Southeast
kernst@ius.edu

Tessue Fields
Associate Professor of Education
Indiana University Southeast
thfields@ius.edu

Kevin Glowacki
Assistant Professor of Classical Studies
Indiana University Bloomington
kglowack@indiana.edu

Elizabeth Goering
Associate Professor of Communication Studies
Indiana University-Purdue University Indianapolis
bgoering@iupui.edu

Sharon Hamilton
Professor of English
Indiana University-Purdue University Indianapolis
shamilto@iupui.edu

Carol Hostetter
Assistant Professor of Social Work
Indiana University Bloomington
chostett@indiana.edu

Jay R. Howard
Associate Professor of Sociology
Indiana University-Purdue University Columbus
howard@iupui.edu

Iztok Hozo
Professor of Mathematics
Indiana University Northwest
ihozo@iun.edu

Dorothy W. Ige
Professor of Communication
Indiana University Northwest
dige@iun.edu

Katherine L. Jackson
Associate Professor of Finance
Indiana University South Bend
kjackson@iusb.edu

Jamie Kauffman
Professor of Speech Communication
Indiana University Southeast
jkauffm@ius.edu

Beth B. Kern
Associate Professor of Accounting
Indiana University South Bend
bkern@iusb.edu

Brenda E. Knowles
Professor of Business Law
Indiana University South Bend
bknowles@iusb.edu

Paul Kochanowski
Professor of Economics
Indiana University South Bend
pkochano@iusb.edu

Keith M. Kovach
Assistant Professor of Technical Graphics
Indiana University-Purdue University Indianapolis
kkovach@iupui.edu

Catherine Larson
Professor of Spanish & Portuguese
Indiana University Bloomington
larson@indiana.edu

Betsy Lucal
Associate Professor of Sociology
Indiana University South Bend
blucal@iusb.edu

Kathleen A. Marrs
Assistant Professor of Biology
Indiana University-Purdue University Indianapolis
kmarrs@iupui.edu

Robin Morgan
Professor of Psychology
Indiana University Southeast
rmorgan@ius.edu

Lori Montalbano-Phelps
Assistant Professor of Communication
Indiana University Northwest
lmontal@iun.edu

Jeannette Nunnelley
Associate Professor of Education
Indiana University Southeast
jnunnell@ius.edu

Robert H. Orr
Professor of Computer Technology
Indiana University-Purdue University Indianapolis
rhorr@iupui.edu

Paul Pittman
Associate Professor of Business Administration
Indiana University Southeast
ppittman@ius.edu

Jerry Powers
Professor Emeritus of Social Work
Indiana University-Purdue University Indianapolis
gpowers@iupui.edu

Elaine Roth
Assistant Professor of English
Indiana University South Bend
elaroth@iusb.edu

Michele C. Russo
Librarian
Indiana University South Bend
mrusso@iusb.edu

Leah Savion
Assistant Professor of Philosophy
Indiana University Bloomington
lsavion@indiana.edu

Stuart Schrader
Assistant Professor of Communication Studies
Indiana University-Purdue University Indianapolis
sschrade@iupui.edu

Scott R. Sernau
Associate Professor of Sociology
Indiana University South Bend
ssernau@iusb.edu

Morteza Shafii-Mousavi
Professor of Mathematics
Indiana University South Bend
mshafii@iusb.edu

S. Holly Stocking
Associate Professor of Journalism
Indiana University Bloomington
stocking@indiana.edu

128

# References

Altman, Howard B. and William E. Cashin. 1992. Writing a syllabus. *Idea Paper* 27. Manhattan: Kansas State University, Division of Continuing Education, Center for Faculty Evaluation and Development.

Angelo, Thomas A., and , K. Patricia Cross. 1993. *Classroom assessment techniques: A handbook for college teachers,* 2d ed. San Francisco: Jossey-Bass.

Astin, Alexander W. 1985. *Achieving educational excellence.* San Francisco: Jossey-Bass.

Austin, Ann E. and Roger G. Baldwin. 1991. *Faculty collaboration: Enhancing the quality of scholarship and teaching.* Washington D.C.: George Washington University Press.

Becker, Angela H. and Sharon K. Calhoon. 1999. What introductory students attend to on a course syllabus. *Teaching of Psychology* 26: 6-11.

Benson, D, Lu Mattson, and Les Adler. 1995. Prompt Feedback. In *The seven principles in action: Improving undergraduate education,* ed. Susan Rickey Hatfield. Bolton, Massachusetts: Anker.

Bloom, Benjamin Samuel, ed. 1956. *Taxonomy of educational objectives; Cognitive domain.* New York: Longmans, Green.

Bonwell, Charles C. and James A. Eison. 1991. Active Learning: Crating Excitement in the Classroom. *ASHE-ERIC Higher Education Report No. 1.* Washington, D.C.: George Washington University, School of Education and Human Development.

Bonwell, Charles and James Eison. 1991. *Active learning: Creating excitement in the classroom.* New York: Wiley Publishing.

Bransford, John D., Ann L.Brown, and Rodney R. Cocking. 2000. *How people learn: Brain, mind, experience and school.* Washington D.C.: National Academy Press; available from http://books.nap.edu/books/0309070368/html/index.html. Accessed 1 July 2003.

Braskamp, Larry A. and John C. Ory. 1994. *Assessing faculty work: Enhancing individual and institutional performance.* San Francisco, CA: Jossey-Bass.

Breivik, Patricia Senn. 1998. *Student learning in the information age.* Phoenix, Arizona: American Council on Education/Oryx Press.

Brookfield, Stephen D. 1995. *Becoming a critically reflective teacher.* San Francisco: Jossey-Bass.

Brooks, Virginia R. 1982. Sex differences in student dominance behavior in female and male professors' classrooms. *Sex Roles* 8: 683-90.

Brophy, Jere E. and Thomas L. Good. 1996. Research in early childhood and /elementary school teaching programs, 3d ed. In *Dynamics of effective teaching,* ed. Richard Kindsvatter, William Willen, and Margaret Ishler. White Plains, New York: Longman.

Brophy, Jere E. 1998. *Motivating students to learn.* Boston: McGraw-Hill.

Bruner, Jerome S. 1966. *Toward a theory of instruction.* Cambridge, Massachusetts: Harvard University Press.

Bybee Roger W., ed. 2002. *Learning science and the science of learning.* Arlington Virginia: National Science Teachers Association.

Caine, Geoffrey, Renate Nummela Caine, and Sam Crowell. 1999. *Mindshifts: A brain-compatible process for professional development and the renewal of education,* 2d ed. Tuscon, Arizona: Zephyr Press.

Caine, Renate Nummela and Geoffrey Caine. 1991. *Making connections: Teaching and the human brain.* Alexandria, Virginia: Association for Supervision and Curriculum Development.

Caine, Renate Nummela and Geoffrey Caine. 1997. *Education on the edge of possibility.* Alexandria, Maryland: Association for Supervision and Curriculum Development.

Caine, Renate Nummela and Geoffrey Caine. 1998. How to think about the brain. *School Administrator* 55, no. 1:12-16.

Caine, Renate Nummela, Geoffrey Caine and Sam Crowell. (1999). *Mindshifts: A braincompatible process for professional development and the renewal of education,* 2d ed. Tuscon, Arizona: Zephyr Press.

Chickering, Arthur and Stephen C. Ehrmann. 1996. Implementing the seven principles: Technology as lever. *AAHE Bulletin* (October): 3-6. Available from http://www.tltgroup.org/programs/seven.html.

Chickering, Arthur W. and Zelda F. Gamson, eds. 1991. *Applying the seven principles for good practice in undergraduate education.* San Francisco: Jossey-Bass.

Chickering, Arthur W. And Zelda F. Gamson. 1987. *Seven principles of good practice in undergraduate education.* Racine, Wisconsin: Johnson Foundation.

Chism, Nancy Van Note. 1999. *Peer review of teaching : A sourcebook.* Bolton, Massachusetts: Anker.

Conlan, Vanessa. 1998. Managing with Class: Effective Classroom Techniques. *The Teaching Professor* 12, no.10.

Constantinople, Ann, Randolph Cornelius and Janet M. Gray. 1988. The chilly climate: fact or artifact? *The Journal of Higher Education* 59: 527-50.

Craik, Fergus I. and Robert S. Lockhart.1972. Levels of processing: A framework for memory research. *Journal of Verbal Learning and Verbal Behavior* 11: 671-684.

Cramer, E. P. 1995. Feminist pedagogy and teaching social work practice with groups: A case study. *Journal of Teaching in Social Work* 11 no.1/2: 193-215.

Crawford, B. 1988. Women and communicative power: *A conceptual approach to communication strategies.* In *Women and communicative power: Theory, research and practice,* ed. Carol A. Valentine and Nancy Hoar. Annandale, Virginia: Speech Communication Association.

Day, Susan. 1989. Producing better writers in sociology classes: A test of the writing-across-the-curriculum approach. *Teaching Sociology* 17: 458-64.

Dewey, John. 1938. *Experience and education.* New York: Macmillian.

Diamond, Marian Clecves and Janet L. Hopson. 1999. *Magic trees of the mind: How to nurture your child's intelligence, creativity, and healthy emotions from birth through adolescence.* New York: Plume.

Driver, Rosalind. 1983. *The pupil as scientist?* Milton Keynes, England: The Open University Press.

Edgerton, Russell, Pat Hutchings, and Kathleen Quinlan. 1991. *The teaching portfolio: Capturing the scholarship in teaching.* Washington, D.C.: American Association for Higher Education.

Enerson, Diane M. 2001. Mentoring as metaphor: An opportunity for innovation and renewal. *New Directions for Teaching and Learning* 85: 7-15.

Evans, Ruby. 2001. Faculty and reference librarians: A virtual dynamic duo. An internal educational partnership for learning. *T.H.E. Journal* 28, no. 6 (Jan): 46, 48-51.

Felder, Richard. 1999. Getting started. *Chemical Engineering Education.* Vol. 29, no. 3: 166-7.

Freire, Paulo. 1970. *Pedagogy of the oppressed.* New York: Seabury.

Freire, Paulo. 1973. *Education for critical consciousness.* New York: Seabury.

Freire, Paulo. 1985. *The politics of education.* New York: Continuum Press.

Fried, Robert.1995. *The passionate teacher*. Boston: Beacon Press.

Gardner, Howard, Mihaly Csikszentmihalyi, and William Damon. 2001. *Good work: When excellence and ethics meet*. New York: Basic Books.

Garmston, Robert. 1997. *The Presenter's fieldbook: A practical guide*. Norwood, Massachusetts: Christopher-Gordon Publishers Inc.

Garside, Colleen. 1996. Look who's talking: A comparison of lecture and group discussion teaching strategies in developing critical thinking skills. *Communication Education* 45: 212- 27.

Gavrin, Andrew A., Kathleen A. Marrs, Robert E. Blake, Jeffrey X. Watt. n.d. WebScience at IUPUI. Indianapolis: Indiana University-Purdue University Indianapolis; available from http://webphysics.iupui.edu/webscience/webscience.html. Accessed 18 August 2003.

Gilson, Caroline and Stephanie Michel. 2002. Fishing for success: faculty/librarian collaboration nets effective library assignments. In *Making the grade: Academic libraries and student success*, ed. Maurie Caitlin Kelly and Andrea Kross. Chicago: Association of College and Research Libraries.

Goffman, Erving. 1963. *Behavior in public places*. New York: Free Press.

Graham, M. A. 1997. Empowering social work faculty: Alternative paradigms for teaching and learning. *Journal of Teaching in Social Work* 15 no.1/2: 33-49.

Grasha, Anthony F. 1996. *Teaching with style: A practical guide to enhancing learning by understanding, teaching and learning styles*. Pittsburgh: Alliance Publishers. Grunert, Judith. 1997. *The course syllabus: A learning-centered approach*. Bolton, MA: Anker Publishing.

Haas, Linda. 1994. Generating discussion from the first day. In *Quick hits: Successful strategies by award winning teachers*, ed. Eileen Bender, Millard Dunn, Bonnie Kendall, Catherine Larson and Peggy Wilkes,12. Bloomington, Indiana: Indiana University Press.

Halpern, Diane F. 1994. *Changing college classrooms: New teaching and learning strategies for an increasingly complex world*. San Francisco, CA: Jossey-Bass.

Harnish, Dorothy and Lynn A.1994. Mentoring strategies for faculty development. *Studies in Higher Education* 19, no.2: 191-201.

Haynes, D. T. and N. C. Bard. 1998. A collaborative teaching model to build competence. *Journal of Teaching in Social Work* 16 no.1/2: 35-55.

Hogue, Dawn.*CyberEnglish9 Policies*. 2003. Sheboygan Falls, Wisconsin: School District of Sheboygan Falls; available from http://www.sheboyganfalls.k12.wi.us/cyberenglish9/

Business/grade%20philosophy.htm. Accessed 15 August 2003.

Howard, Jay R. and Amanda L. Henney. 1998. Student participation and instructor gender in the mixed age college classroom. *The Journal of Higher Education* 69: 384-405.

Howard, Jay R. and Roberta Baird. 2000. The consolidation of responsibility and students' definitions of the college classroom. *The Journal of Higher Education* 71: 700-721.

Howard, Jay R., George James and David R. Taylor. 2002. The consolidation of responsibility in the mixed-age college classroom. *Teaching Sociology* 30, no. 2: 214-234.

Howard, Jay R., Lillard B. Short and Susan M. Clark. 1996. Student participation in the mixed-age college classroom. *Teaching Sociology* 24: 8-24.

Huerta, Deborah and Victoria E. McMillan. 2000. Collaborative instruction by writing and library faculty: A two-tiered approach to the teaching of scientific writing. *Issues in Science & Technology Librarianship* 28 (Fall).

Hunt, Nancy P. and Roy M. Bohlin. 1995. Events and practices that promote attitudes and emotions in computing courses. *Journal of Computing in Teaching Education* 11, no. 3 (Spring): 21-2.

Jensen, E. 2000. *Brain-based learning*, rev. ed. San Diego, California: The Brain Store.

Jensen, Eric. 1998. *Introduction to brain-compatible learning*. San Diego, California: The Brain Store.

Jensen, Eric. 1998. *Teaching with the brain in mind*. Alexandria, Virginia: Association for Supervision and Curriculum Development.

Johnson, David W., Roger T. Johnson and Karl A. Smith. 1991. Cooperative learning: increasing college faculty instructional productivity. *ASHE_ERIC Higher Education Report No. 4*. Washington, D.C.: George Washington University.

Karp, David A. and William C. Yoels. 1976. The college classroom: Some observation on the meaning of student participation. *Sociology and Social Research* 60: 421-39.

Kember, David. 2000. *Action learning and action research: Improving the quality of teaching and learning*. London: Kogan Page.

Kember, David and Lyn Gow. 1994. Orientations to teaching and their effect on the quality of student learning. *Journal of Higher Education* 65: 58-74.

Kindsvatter, Richard, William Willen, and Margaret Ishler. 1996. *Dynamics of effective teaching*, 3d ed. Wite Plains, New York: Longman.

Knowles, Malcolm Shepherd. 1980. *The modern practice of adult education from pedagogy to andragogy.* New York: Cambridge.

Kohn, Alfie. 1993. Punished by rewards: *The trouble with gold stars, incentive plans, A's, praise, and other bribes.* New York: Houghton Mifflin.

Laker, Ken and Philip D. Farnum. 2001. *EE441 and EE442: EE Senior Design, 2000-2001.* Philadephia: University of Pennsylvania; available from http://www.seas.upenn.edu/ ese/ee442/presentations/vgexample/VGexample.pdf. Accessed 15 August 2003

Lang, P., M. Little,, and V. Cronen. 1990. The systemic professional domains of action and the question of neutrality. *Human Systems: The Journal of Systemic Consultation and Management* 1: 39-55.

Latzko, William J. and David M. Saunders. 1995. *Four Days with Dr. Deming: A strategy for modern methods of management..* Reading, MA: Addison-Wesley.

Lavington, Camille. 1997. *You've only got three seconds.* New York: Doubleday Press.

LeClercq, Terri. 1999. Seven Principles for Good Practice in Legal Education: Principle 4: Good Practice Gives Prompt Feedback. *Journal of Legal Education* 49, no.3: 418-29.

Leonard, William H. 1997 How do College Students Learn Science? In *Methods of effective teaching and course management for university and college science teachers,* ed. by Eleanor D. Siebert, Mario W. Caprio, Carri M. Lyda. Dubuque Iowa: Kendall-Hunt Publishers.

Light, Greg and Roy Cox. 2001. *Learning and teaching in higher education: The reflective professional.* Thousand Oaks, CA: Sage.

Lipton, Laura and Bruce M. Wellman. 1998. *Pathways to understanding: Patterns and practices in the learning-focused classroom.* Guilford, Vermont: Pathways Publishing.

Lyons, Richard E., Meggin McIntosh and Marcella L. Kysilka.. 2003. *Teaching college in an age of accountability.* Boston: Allyn and Bacon.

MacDonald, D. and G. Issacs. 2001. Developing a professional identity through problem based learning. *Teaching Education* 12, no. 3: 315-333.

Margrath, William. 2001. A Return to Interactivity: The Third Wave in Educational Uses of Information Technology. *CALICO Journal* 18, no. 2: 283-94.

Marrs, Kathleen A. *Biology 540 -- Topics in Biotechnology. 2003.* Indianapolis: Indiana University-Purdue University Indianapolis, Department of Biology; available at http://www.biology.iupui.edu/biocourses/Biol540/. Accessed 18 August 2003.

Marrs, Kathleen A. 2003. *Biology N100: Contemporary Biology, Winter / Spring 2003.* Indianapolis: Indiana University-Purdue University Indianapolis, Department of Biology; available from http://www.biology.iupui.edu/biocourses/N100/. Accessed 18 August 2003.

Marrs, Kathleen A. and G. Novak. 2003. Just-in-time teaching in biology: Creating an active learner classroom using the internet. *(Cell Biology Education*, forthcoming).

McKeachie, Wilbert J. 1990. Research on college teaching: The historical background. *Journal of Educational Psychology* 82: 189-200.

Marrs Kathleen A., Robert E. Blake, and Andrew.D Gavrin. 2003. Use of Warm up exercises in just in time teaching: Determining students' prior knowledge and misconceptions in biology, chemistry, and physics. *(Journal of College Science Teaching*, forthcoming).

Maxwell Rhoda J. 1996. *Writing across the curriculum in middle and high schools.* Boston: Allyn & Bacon.

McKeachie, Wilbert J. 1994. *Teaching tips: Strategies, research, and theory for college and university teachers*. 9th ed. Lexington, Massachusetts: D.C. Heath.

McKeachie, Wilbert J. 1994. *Teaching tips: A guide book for the beginning college teacher*, 9th ed. Lexington, Massachusetts: Heath.

Meyers, Chet and Thomas B. Jones. 1993. *Promoting active learning: Strategies for the college classroom*. San Francisco: Jossey-Bass.

Nagda, Biren A., Margaret L. Spearmon, Lynn C. Holley, Scott Harding, Mary Lou Balassone, Dominique Moise-Swanson and Stan de Mello. 1999. Intergroup dialogues: An innovative approach to teaching about diversity and justice in social work programs. *Journal of Social Work Education* 35 no. 3: 433-449.

Novak, G. 2003. *Just-in-time teaching*. Indianapolis: Indiana University-Purdue University Indianapolis; available from http://webphysics.iupui.edu/jitt/jitt.html. Accessed 18 August 2003.

Novak, Gregor M., E. T. Patterson, Andrew D. Gavrin, and W. Christian. 1999. *Just-in-time teaching: Blending active learning with web technology*. Upper Saddle River, New Jersey: Prentice Hall.

Novak, Joseph Donald. 1987. *Proceedings of the second international seminar on misconceptions and educational strategies in science and mathematics, July 26-29, 1987, Cornell University, Ithaca, NY, USA*. New York: Cornell University.

Nunn, Claudia E. 1996. Discussion in the college classroom: Triangulating observational and survey results. *The Journal of Higher Education* 67: 243-66.

135

Orr, Robert H., Margaret Applegate, Mark Grove, Sandy Hellyer, Norman Douglas Lees and Kimberly Quaid. 1995. Report on Grade Inflation at IUPUI. Indianapolis: Indiana University Purdue University Indianapolis.

Osborne, Roger and P. S. Freyberg. 1985. *Learning in science: The implications of children's science*. Auckland, New Zealand: Heinemann.

Palmer, Parker. 1998. *The courage to teach: Exploring the inner landscape of a teacher's life*. San Francisco, California: Jossey-Bass.

Parkes, Jay and Mary B. Harris. 2002. The purpose of a syllabus. *College Teaching* 50: 55-61.

Parry, Terence and Gayle Gregory. 1998. *Designing brain compatible learning*. Arlington Heights, Illinois: Skylight Training and Publishing, Inc.

Pearce, W. Barnett. 1994. *Interpersonal communication: Making social worlds*. New York: Harper Collins Press.

Perlman, B. & McCann, L. 1999. Student perspectives on the first day of class. *Faculty Forum*, Vol. 26, no. 4.

Petronio, S. 1999. "Translating scholarship into practice": An alternative metaphor. *Journal of Applied Communication* 27: 87-91.

Pierce, Gloria. 1998. Developing new university faculty through mentoring. *Journal of Humanistic Education and Development* 37, no.1: 27-40.

Raspa, Dick and Dane Ward, eds. 2000. *The collaborative imperative: Librarians and faculty working together in the information universe*. Chicago: Association of College and Research Libraries.

Rau, William and Ann Durand. 2000. The academic ethic and college grades: Does hard work help students to "make the grade"? *Sociology of Education* 73: 19-38.

Raymark, Patrick H. and Patricia A. Connor-Green. 2002. The syllabus quiz. *Teaching of Psychology* 29: 286-288.

Rieman, Patricia L. 2000. *Teaching portfolios: Presenting your professional best*. Boston: McGraw Hill.

Rudd, Rima E. and John P. Comings. 1994. Learner developed materials: an empowering product. *Health Education Quarterly* 21 no.3: 313-327.

Schramm, Peter W. 1999. *The Meaning of Grades*. Ashland, Ohio: Ashland University; available from http://www.ashland.edu/colleges/arts_sci/polysci/syllabi/1999fall/ 101_ schramm.html. Accessed 15 August 2003.

Seldin, Peter. 1993. *Successful Use of Teaching Portfolios*. Bolton, Massachusetts: Anker.

Senge, Peter M.. 2000. *Schools that learn: A fifth discipline fieldbook for educators, parents, and everyone who cares about education*. New York: Doubleday Press.

Shafii-Mousavi, Morteza and Ken Smith. 2002. *Interdepartmental Collaborations for a Community of Teaching and Learning*. Academic Chairpersons: The Changing Role of Department Chairs, National Issues in Higher Education Series 52: 177-184.

Shafii-Mousavi, Morteza and Paul Kochanowski. 2000. How to design and teach a project based first-year finite mathematics course. *The Journal of Undergraduate Mathematics and Its Applications (UMAP)* 21, no. 2: 119-138.

Shafii-Mousavi, Morteza and Paul Kochanowski. 1999. The use of computer technology in a first-year finite mathematics course. In *Mathematics/Science Education Technology*, Charlottesville, Virginia: Association for Advancement of Computing in Education.

Silberman, Melvin L. 1996. *Active learning: 101 strategies to teach any subject*. Boston: Allyn and Bacon.

Smith, Daryl G. 1977. College classroom interactions and critical thinking. *Journal of Educational Psychology* 69: 180-90.

Smith, Mary F. and Nabil Y. Razzouk. 1993. Improving classroom communication: the case of the course syllabus. *Journal of Education for Business* 68: 215-221.

Sorcinelli, Mary D. 1994. Effective approaches to new faculty development. *Journal of Counseling and Development* 72, no. 5: 474-480.

Sousa, David A. 1995. *How the brain learns: A classroom teacher's guide*. Reston, Virginia: National Association of Secondary School Principals.

Sousa, David A. 2001. *How the brain learns: A Classroom teacher's guide,*. 2d ed. Thousand Oaks, California: Corwin Press.

St. Clair, Karen L. 1994. Faculty-to-faculty mentoring in the community college: An instructional component of faculty. *Community College Review* 22, no.3: 23-36.

Steen, Sarah, Chris Bader and Charis Kubrin. 1999. Rethinking the graduate seminar. *Teaching Sociology* 27: 167-173.

Stipek, Deborah. 1998. *Motivation to learn : From theory to practice*, 3d ed. Boston: Allyn and Bacon.

Sylwester, Robert. 2000. Unconscious emotions, conscious feelings. *Educational Leadership* 58, no. 3: 20-24.

Tileston, Donna Walker. 2000. *10 best teaching practices: how brain research, learning styles, and standards define teaching competencies*. Thousand Oaks, California: Corwin Press.

Timpson, William, Suzanne Burgoyne, Christine Jones and Waldo Jones. 1997. Teaching and performing: Ideas for energizing you classes. Madison, Wisconsin: Magna Publications.

Undergraduate Studies Committee, Faculty of Environmental Studies. 1984. *Guidelines to the Meaning of Grades*. Waterloo, Ontario Canada: University of Waterloo; available from http://www.ahs.uwaterloo.ca/~jthomson/grade.html. Accessed 15 August, 2003.

Wald, Penelope and Michael Castleberry. 2000. *Educators as Learners: Creating a Professional Learning Community in Your School*. Association for Supervision and Curriculum Development, Alexandria, Virginia.

Walvoord, B.E., B. Bardes and J. Denton. 1998. Closing the feedback loop in classroom-based assessment. *Assessment Update* 10 no.5: 1-4.

Weimer, Maryellen and Rose Ann Neff, eds. 1990. *Teaching college: Collected readings for the new instructor*. Madison, Wisconsin: Magna Publications.

Williams, Bev. 2001. The theoretical links between problem-based learning and self directed learning for continuing professional nursing education. *Teaching in Higher Education* 6, no. 1: 85-98.

Wolfe, Patricia. 2001. *Brain matters: Translating research into classroom practice*. Alexandria, Virginia: Association for Supervision and Curriculum Development.

# Subject Index

(Page numbers refer to beginning page of the article in which a topic is discussed.)